RED WELLS

To Gug
with Best Wishes
Sharon Wells Wagner

Cover art and design by Steve Wagner,
Alias Entertainment

ISBN: 1-4196-4115-8
Library of Congress Control Number: 2006906892

Published by BookSurge Publishing
Charleston, South Carolina

To order additional copies, please contact us.
BookSurge, LLC
www.booksurge.com
1-866-308-6235
orders@booksurge.com

SHARON WELLS
WAGNER

RED WELLS
An American Soldier in World War II
And the
99th Infantry Battalion (Separate),
The Viking Battalion

A Life Story

2006

RED WELLS

TABLE OF CONTENTS

God loves us no matter what we have done;
His love does not change.
He forgives us for everything if we confess with a humble
heart.

J. David Wagner

ACKNOWLEDGMENTS

I never suffered this war until I wrote this book, but only through the eyes of the storyteller, my Father. This is his story, and he willingly told it so that his children and grandchildren would know. Along with the joys of writing came the anguish of knowing, and for him, the anguish of remembering and reliving. There were many sad memories, but it wasn't always difficult, for we had a lot of laughs along the way.

The evolution of this book, as with any book, was a process. It began when I was a child. As we were growing up, my Father told us many stories about the war—some amusing, others amazing—so naturally I developed an interest. However, attending the World War II Memorial Dedication Ceremony in Washington, D.C. with my Father in May, 2004, piqued my interest in the war, and suddenly I needed to know. I needed more than pieces; I wanted the whole pie. I wanted to understand what part he played in this historic conflict. So that's how it came to pass; my Father had lived the story, and I loved to write! Thanks, Dad, for making our book possible!

Thank you, Rick Wagner, my resident historian, genealogist, and World War II enthusiast, who also happens to be my husband of 32 years. He drew the maps for the book and was gracious in sharing his knowledge of our family's history and of WWII by willingly filling in holes that were difficult for me to fill.

Steve Wagner, my son, assisted in editing parts of the manuscript, proofread the finished product, and designed the beautiful book cover. Thanks for a job well done. I love you!

My daughter, Stephanie Wagner, willingly and patiently sat and listened to many readings so that I could hear the stories and get a feel for where I was going with them. Her feedback was important, and her facial expressions spoke volumes! Thanks! I love you, sweet pea!

Thank you, Helen Wells Stephenson, my sister in spirit and in life, for *knowing,* sharing, and listening, and most important of all, for all your encouragement and inspiration when I needed it most.

Thank you Kathleen Wagner for your unending support and encouragement, and for always "lighting the way..."

Thank you Beatrice Arnold Wells for the wonderful pictures and for sharing stories about our family.

A special thanks to Roy Francia, my publicist, for introducing me to the world of publishing and for simplifying my transition from writer to author. It's been a pleasure working with you!

Thanks to my editor, Kenneth Broadway, John Schuster, and Lindsay Parker of BookSurge for your patience and expertise. Thank you sincerely for a job well done.

Thank you David Oustad, son of Arne Oustad of the 99th Infantry Battalion (Separate), for graciously providing a copy of *Company D,* United States Army, by Sgt. John Kelly, when it was impossible to find. Thanks, too, for permitting me to publish your father's photo in RED WELLS. It meant a lot to us. Tusen takk!

Thank you, Bill Hoffland, son of Joseph Hoffland of the 99th Infantry Battalion (Separate), for granting me permission to use the wonderful photos from the 99th web site; and a special thanks to all the 99ers and their families who graciously allowed the photos to be published in RED WELLS. Tusen takk!

Thank you, Jarvis Taylor, Company D of the 99th Infantry Battalion (Separate), for permitting me to use your wonderful photos. Tusen takk!

Helen,

My Beloved Wife Of 52 Years,
Who Always Wanted Me
To Write My Story.
Je Elsker Dig
Your Bobby

* * *

Red Wells

Daddy,
Thank You For The Gift Of
Service To Our Country,
And Thank You
For The Gift Of Your Story
So That Others May Know, And Feel, And Remember.

Mom,
For All The Fun We Had

Rick
For Always Being There

Steve & Stephanie
Because I Love You

* * *

Sharon Wells Wagner

INTRODUCTION

My father, Red Wells, and I wrote this book together. Nearly every morning for almost a year, we sat at my computer, took scenic drives in the country, relaxed by our favorite fishing hole too absorbed in the past to watch our lines, or lounged on my deck, our feet propped on the railing as the sun streamed through the branches of my favorite willow tree. He regaled me with stories as I typed, tape recorded, or hand wrote frantically just trying to keep up. We laughed and we cried. We even picked up a couple of guitars on occasion and sang *Old Shep* and *The Boardinghouse,* following along with the words on my computer screen, until we were delirious with laughter, becoming completely unproductive for the rest of the day.

We argued over the words to *In Flanders' Fields,* my father's favorite poem, after he recited it from memory. We were always drunk on coffee, talking a mile a minute. I'd grind fresh beans on the espresso setting and brew a whole pot, and sometimes we'd brew a second. When I became chair bound for the next four months due to a badly broken ankle, the telephone became our medium. New stories and fascinating details flowed into my ears, down through my arms and fingers and onto the keyboard. Nothing could stop us; we were on a roll! It was exhilarating and mesmerizing, joyful and painful, but mostly just plain wonderful, much like the joy of anticipating Christmas.

I had always wanted to write a book. A book is a legacy. A legacy to the future, to someone who might pick it up and do something good with it and, of course, learn something from it. So it occurred to me in mid August of 2005 that I really wanted to write the story of my Dad's life, especially his service in the Army. I approached him, and he agreed. He had always wanted to "write it down," so I said, "Daddy, let's do it," and we started the very next day.

It wasn't always easy for my Dad to talk about the war. Over the years I had heard many stories, but I always knew there were more. I'd heard stories about twenty mile hikes with heavy back packs, guarding the Panama Canal with a sawed-off shotgun, or being shaken from his cot by a rumbling volcano in the Aleutian Islands. Stories about huge boa constrictors in the jungles of Trinidad, a dog named AWOL, and an ornery mule named Devil. I knew my Dad could fly a plane, had parachuted over England, and once landed in a tree. I knew he loved the Norwegian people and stood proudly as Honor Guard to their king. I was in awe of the whole thing.

I also knew that he fired at and was fired upon by the enemy. He was awarded a Bronze Star and a Combat Infantry Badge. But these were the stories untold, clandestine involvements that were tucked away forever. The horrors of war are always repressed in the hope that they will be forgotten. But in the early spring of 2004, when my Dad was 81 years old, something happened that made it okay for him to talk more freely about the war.

Early in April, I read in my local newspaper that there was going to be an official dedication ceremony for the new World War II Memorial in Washington, D.C. on Memorial Day Weekend. I had been unaware of this event but moved quickly in an effort to get tickets. However, the tickets were gone and had been for many months. I really wanted to take my Dad to this dedication and was determined to make it happen. I knew it would mean a lot to him, so I sent an email to the White House, addressed directly to President George W. Bush, and gave him a brief summery of my Dad's military service. A few weeks later, four tickets arrived in my mailbox. We were given seats in the MCI Center—the best seats in the house. From there, we could watch the entire dedication ceremony in air conditioning and enjoy an exclusive live celebration of the war era.

Phone calls were made, a hotel was booked, and a scooter was rented for my Dad so he could navigate the Mall and visit all the sights. My son, Steve, joined us on our jaunt to the nation's capitol. The dedication was held on the 29th of May, so we drove to Washington on the morning of the 28th.

I made a sign for my Dad's scooter, which he proudly displayed. It designated his battalion, the 99th Infantry Battalion (Separate). He wore an embroidered hat with the emblem his unit and was dressed in a navy blue sport coat with his Bronze Star and Combat Infantry Badge pinned to the lapel. It was his hope that someone from his battalion would be in attendance and recognize him. Instead, he drew the attention of several WWII historians. One man, who we met on the Mall, was there specifically to meet and speak with the veterans. He saw my Dad's hat, shook his hand, and proceeded to tell us about the 99th Infantry Battalion (Separate), how important it was and how elite it was. In his words, they were the first Green Berets. They were special troops who were used for very difficult and dangerous assignments. Hearing that opened my eyes. I knew all along that my Dad was very proud to be a member of this battalion, but I never really knew why. Now I was starting to understand.

All of the veterans were treated like royalty. When we entered the MCI Center, the staff greeted us like they knew us personally, shook my Dad's hand, thanked him profusely for his service, and then escorted us to our seats. Veterans in wheelchairs or on scooters were given front row seating.

While waiting for the show to begin, we were approached by another World War II historian who was also a Navy commander in charge of a training vessel. He had brought with him some of his young charges to meet and talk with the veterans. He spotted the emblem on my Dad's hat, got very excited, and began speaking to my Dad in Norwegian. My Dad's eyes lit up, and he answered the man in Norwegian. The commander was amazed to meet someone from the 99th, and he couldn't stop talking to my Dad and asking him questions about it. Here sat my Dad—a living piece of history. He was there, he saw it, and he lived it. The man was just amazed.

The commander introduced his men to my Dad and gave them a brief education about his experiences with the 99th. They each proudly shook his hand. Then he emphatically informed us of the significance and eliteness of this small battalion. I was hearing it all over again.

The show at the MCI center was a dramatic reenactment of World War II. It was very intense and emotional and evoked powerful memories, both poignant and painful. But out of this came an understanding of why we were at war, what we did in this war, and why it was necessary and important to bring it to a close. After more than six decades, the wounds could finally start to heal.

Attending the dedication opened my eyes to a lot of things I didn't realize about WWII—its sheer magnitude and consequence was overwhelming. It was an emotional experience for me. My Dad said it was "one of the happiest days and also one of the saddest days" of his life.

I know this event made it easier for my Dad to talk about the war and fostered my need to know more about my Dad's involvement in the war. We formed an even closer bond for having shared this experience. And out of good experiences come good things—our book! Thanks, Dad, for making this book possible. I know it will be a success, and we will be proud of it, in much the same way that I am proud of you!

Sharon Wells Wagner

THE 99TH INFANTRY BATTALION (SEPARATE)
The Viking Battalion

"There was a comradery among us,
a fellowship unlike any I had ever known..."

The 99th Infantry Battalion (Separate) was a battalion made up of Norwegian nationals and American-born Norwegians. It was called the Viking Battalion and was conceived in 1942 and organized at Camp Ripley in Minnesota the same year. The battalion consisted of nearly 900 men who were trained at Fort Snelling, Minnesota and Camp Hale, Colorado for use in covert operations in occupied Norway. They received very specialized commando training during harsh winter conditions. They were trained as paratroopers and mountain climbers. They knew how to ski and spoke flawless Norwegian, as well as English.

They were carefully chosen and highly trained to invade and liberate Norway. Norway was the origin of their roots and many had family still living there. For some, it was home. The men held a strong allegiance to this land, and they were ready to reclaim it from the enemy.

This battalion was separate, meaning they were not attached to any larger unit, nor were they, by any means, regular. They were elite, highly trained troops that would be used for very special assignments. They eventually traveled to England and Wales, where they received more training.

In the spring of 1943 the feasibility of troops going into occupied Norway was re-evaluated and deemed counterproductive at that time due to possible repercussions against the Norwegian people. However, a small contingent of 99ers volunteered to participate in covert raids in Norway. The remaining 800 men left for Omaha Beach, Normandy, and the front lines. They were often split up and sent out on separate missions but always came back together as a battalion.

This famous battalion had its origins in Minnesota, but its legendary activities began in Europe when it landed in Normandy on June 22, 1944. Its first mission was the battle raging in Cherbourg, where it first saw combat and suffered its first casualties of the war. Here is where my father, Red Wells, came to the 99th. He was a volunteer replacement, a highly trained infantry soldier. He joined them willingly at Cherbourg, stayed with them throughout the European Theatre of Operations, and went with them to Norway, at the close of the war, to disarm and repatriate 350,000 German soldiers and high-ranking officers.

The battalion's finale was an honorable and much deserved one: they welcomed home their own King, Haakon VII, who had been five years in exile in England. My Father had the great honor to stand before the King as a member of his Honor Guard. After their work in Norway was finished, some of the 99th stayed there with family, some married Norwegian women, and the rest of them went home. The end of World War II brought to a conclusion the activities of one of the finest battalions in the history of the United States Army, but their story will forever live on.

PART ONE

1

The Beginning

I was born on the second day of August, or perhaps the third, in the year 1923. No one is really quite sure; there is no documented proof. My birth took place in a small bungalow on a wooded hillside in Fritztown, Berks County, Pennsylvania. My mother, Eva, lived there with my father, Harry, and their children, all seven of them. Eight, if you counted little Dolly who died of pneumonia a few months after birth and was buried in the back yard. My half-siblings, Frances, Charles, Catharine and Thomas, were the children of my mother's marriage to Charles Brice. Their father was a young man who died in the flu epidemic of 1918. I was the second born of my real siblings, Betty and John.

My father was a tinsmith, well-respected in his trade, who mostly put tin roofs on old farm houses. He was very gifted at turning the tin into a variety of items and was a skilled carpenter as well. The house we lived in was built entirely by hand, his hand, with no help from anyone else. His talents were well known and kept him very busy and away a lot of the time. My mother, on the other hand, stayed home and took care of her children.

By early 1925, when I was a year and a half of age, old enough to be toddling around on my own, I was still unable to walk. Of course, I was too young to remember this. Early that year my sisters and brothers took me out for a ride on the sled. We had an accident that involved a tree, and I was injured and taken to a hospital. During this brief hospital visit it was discovered that I had tuberculosis of the bones in my spine. My mother finally understood why I was never able to walk. She was given the sad news that I would have to be hospitalized for a very long time. It was my only hope for a complete recovery. I would never get to know my mother or experience the love and security of growing up in a family that most kids take for granted. She had no choice but to send me away.

My earliest memories are of my mother, father and sister, Betty, coming down to visit me at a crippled children's hospital in Atlantic City, New Jersey. I was about three years old at the time. Hospital rules were strict and permitted only one visitor at a time, so the others would wait outside on the beach. I felt like I was being visited by strangers, not much different than the staff that tended me regularly at the hospital. Occasionally my mom or dad was permitted to visit me in my room, but usually I was wheeled to a balcony where I could see my family on the beach below. Because I wore a large cumbersome cast and was bedridden, the nurses rolled my bed out onto a large porch which faced the ocean, and I would wave to my family. I vividly remember watching them waving to me.

During my years in the hospital, I rarely saw my mother or father. They split up, and my father stopped visiting me. My mother didn't have a car and was too poor to travel to Atlantic City, so I rarely saw her anymore after that. If it hadn't been for the staff at the hospital, I wouldn't have known who my parents were. I was told to "wave to your mother and father," and did as I was instructed. It didn't really matter to me; I had no idea at that time what was missing in my life. Later on, however, I would miss them both greatly.

Life during those days in the hospital was monotonous, filled mostly with discomfort and boredom. The staff always treated me kindly, but I have no recollections of ever being entertained, and certainly never receiving any kind of education.

I was eventually transferred to a crippled children's hospital in Elizabethtown, Pennsylvania. I had made some progress and would now be closer to home. Many of my early childhood memories have faded away, but I have some recollections of life in the hospital in Elizabethtown. Dr. Bisbing visited me there; he was the only person with whom I felt a connection and I looked forward to his visits. I also remember the cast that went up my entire left leg and completely around my waist. It was uncomfortable and confining. Years later after I recovered and went home, I made up for all those years in confinement.

Dr. Bisbing diagnosed my tuberculosis shortly after the sledding accident and took great interest in my case and in me as well. He was a caring man who visited me in the hospital as often as his busy schedule permitted. He occasionally took me home for a visit with my mother, stopping along the way to buy groceries for her. He was a kind and compassionate man with a heart large enough to love every downtrodden, sick or poor human being he ever met. I was one of many. After a brief visit at home, he'd take me back to the hospital.

Because of his kindness, I formed a bond with him and looked forward to his visits. This bond was the only family-like experience I ever had as a child. Later in my life, when WWII was over, I looked him up, and we kept in touch until he passed away many years later.

When I was about eight years old, I was transferred to Mt. Alto Tubercular Sanitarium near Gettysburg, Pennsylvania, where I stayed for about a year. I was recovering nicely and began walking for the first time in my life. Learning to walk was a slow and difficult process, but I was determined to succeed in completely overcoming my handicap. Over the next couple of years I would eventually walk normally.

When I finally came home from the hospital in 1932, I was still wearing a brace on my left leg that went up and around my waist, which was confining and made walking very difficult. As the train pulled into the Outer Station in Reading, my mother and sister, Betty, were there to greet me. Also waiting there were Dr. Bisbing and his nurse. I was fond of her because she had red hair like me. After stepping off the train, I went over to the only familiar faces on the platform: Dr. Bisbing and his nurse. Sadly, I did not acknowledge my own mother or sister because I did not recognize them.

Dr. Bisbing drove us home in his big beautiful car that afternoon, first stopping at 5th and Penn Streets to buy us soft pretzels. It wouldn't surprise me if he had brought along groceries, as well, for my mother as he had done on many prior occasions. I was back in my hometown now but would have to spend some time in the Berks County Tuberculosis Sanitarium before I could go home to my mother. Finally, in the spring of my tenth year the staff declared me well enough to go home and discharged me to the care of my mother. It was 1933, and I would have little more than a year to get to know her.

2
My Mother

In the spring of 1933 when I was discharged from the tuberculosis sanitarium, I went home to live with my mother, sister, Betty, and brother, Tommy. Because my time at home was so brief, I don't have many memories of my mother except that she was poor, very kind to everyone, and always helped others in need. She was well liked by everyone who knew her. In later years any mention of her was done with great love and admiration. Even though I was mischievous and didn't obey her, she was kind to me and forgiving, scolding me gently only occasionally. She scrubbed floors and did general housekeeping chores at a local doctor's office for a dollar a day and brought scrap paper home for me and my sister, Betty, because we liked to draw.

Because our mother worked long hours for so little money, Tommy and I helped her by selling chewing gum and daily newspapers in front of the Capitol Theater at 340 Penn Street (formerly the Grand Opera House). We'd buy a couple boxes of chewing gum from a wholesale tobacco dealer on Penn Street, and then we'd go to the newspaper office across the street and buy a bundle of newspapers. We were very resourceful salesmen and were usually sold out in a very short time. Tommy handled all the money because I couldn't count change. This was my first summer at home, and I hadn't started school yet. All the money we earned we took home to our mother.

We often went to the Elks Home at Fifth and Franklin Streets and sold gum and newspapers to the old guys who were sitting outside in the yard. They had great sympathy for me because I was crippled, and they always bought us out completely. I found out later in life that the Elks had paid for my brace and some of my medical expenses when I was hospitalized.

By age eleven I finally came to know my maternal grandparents. Visiting my mother's parents was a big deal to me. We'd walk to my grandparents' home on 17-1/2 Street in East Reading from our small house on Wood Street in the city. My grandmother prepared wonderful home cooked meals for us. They were kind and loving people who treated us well. They grew all kinds of vegetables in their big backyard garden and always gave some to my mother to take home.

Betty and I went door to door selling my grandparents' fresh vegetables in the neighborhood. We were welcomed by everyone and had to make frequent trips to the garden to replenish our supplies. Visiting with the neighbors and earning a little money was a lot of fun for us. We turned the money over to our grandparents who in turn rewarded us for our efforts. I'm certain they gave some money to my mother as well.

We kids occasionally spent the night at our grandparents' house. My mother put us on the trolley on Penn Street and we hopped off at 18th Street and walked the rest of the way. This was the 'big time'—going to our grandparents' house to spend the night!

My grandfather, Albert J. Roland, was born in 1857 and was nearly 75 years old the summer I came to know him. He seemed very ancient to me. My grandmother, Susan Linseman Roland, who was born in 1868, was eleven years his junior and the more energetic of the pair. They married on April 7, 1888 and had four children, Anna Roland Doyle, Mary (Margaret) Roland Hoffman, James Roland and my mother, Eva.

Mother's sister, Margaret, with whom I would eventually live, was a kind and loving person. I don't remember mother's sister Anna, but Mother's brother, Jim, who had served in WWI as an infantry soldier, had made quite an impression on me. He was gassed during the war which left him somewhat mentally disabled. He was fond of me and after my service as an infantry soldier in WWII referred to me as his dough boy, which is what infantry soldiers were called during WWI.

Grandfather's father was Albert R. Roland, and his mother was Catharine Lotz Roland whose parents owned a hat factory in Adamstown in the mid 1800^s. The Lotz Hat Factory made fine quality woolen hats. As a young man, Grandfather became a hat maker, most likely having learned his trade in his Grandfather Lotz's hat factory.

The few memories I have of our brief time together are very fond ones. My grandfather died shortly after I came to know him. My grandmother lived on for another fifteen years until she eventually passed away in the winter of 1949. My mother was born of good people; they were kind and had a strong sense of family. I am proud of them all.

3
Aunt Laura

My mother left my father some time during the years that I was away in the hospital. It didn't matter much to me because I hardly knew either one of them. Even though I was living with my mother now, I maintained some contact with my father. My sister, Betty, and I visited him occasionally at a church on 5th Street, and he gave us a little spending money. I believe he was a good person even though I never got to know him well. I was often told that I looked just like him, especially when I smoked my corn cob pipe. He was tough, a survivor, and I am probably a lot more like him than I realize.

My mother had moved from my father's house in rural Fritztown to a small row house in the 100 block of Wood Street, in Reading. About a year after I left the hospital and moved in with her, the landlord evicted us because my mother could no longer afford to pay the rent. She worked hard from morning till night scrubbing floors but still didn't earn enough to support us. I remember when the landlord put our furniture out on the front sidewalk. My mother was devastated. Soon after, we packed up everything and moved to an apartment on South 7th Street in the same city. Life was tough for my mother and she soon became ill and went into the hospital. Once again I was separated from her and only saw her occasionally after that.

My Aunt Laura took me in. Laura Spencer, my father's sister, was an immaculate, no-nonsense woman who ran a boarding house at 10th and Cherry Streets in Reading. Although slightly overweight, she was agile and swift and didn't take crap from anybody, especially not from me. Because she was strict, I resisted her rules and provoked her constantly even though each indiscretion earned me a whack from the broom she wielded like a weapon. She kept me busy in the kitchen washing dishes, chopping vegetables and cleaning off tables. A chubby, middle aged woman named Rosie, who was a friend of Aunt Laura, did a lot of the cooking, and my chores were a bit more tolerable when she was around. She was kind to me and kept me out of trouble to the best of her ability.

Aunt Laura was a very good cook, who made huge kettles of homemade soups, chili, fried chicken, and the best crab cakes in town. Her daughter, Anna, helped her in the kitchen, and together, with Rosie, they cooked three meals a day, complete with all the trimmings, enough for her family, every one of her boarders, and all of the local folks who appreciated a good home cooked meal. The locals were her regulars, and at twenty-five cents a plate, she had a steady income. Those wonderful home cooked meals were served family style in the front room of the boardinghouse and were a big hit. Meals were available seven days a week, and there was never a shortage of food or regulars. Aunt Laura's chili was a favorite, especially for me.

The produce Aunt Laura used to make her famous soups came straight from the farm. She owned a small place just outside of town where she grew tomatoes, potatoes and other vegetables for her boarding house. She also had a flock of chickens that provided fresh meat and dozens of eggs for her hungry tenants. There was a small house and a barn on the property with lots of room to grow the fresh produce she needed. A single, middle-aged man, whose name I can no longer recall, lived there on the farm as caretaker and was responsible for feeding the chickens and tending the gardens.

Aunt Laura owned a car, a beautiful 1936 Buick roadster with a wooden steering wheel. She did not drive, so two or three times a week her daughter, Anna, would drive her down to the farm to gather up some fresh supplies. Often they took me along on these trips. I enjoyed the farm, especially the chickens, and it was a chance to go for a ride in the car.

Sometimes just Anna and I went to the farm, and she let me drive the car. Aunt Laura didn't know that just outside of town, Anna would pull the car over and I would slide into the driver's seat. Now remember, I was just 12 years old, a little young to drive, but I learned very quickly to shift gears and was able to handle that big roadster in no time at all.

Unbeknownst to anyone in the house, I took the Buick one afternoon and drove it all the way through town and out to the country for a visit with my friends, the Lorahs. The family came out of the house to greet me when I pulled up. They had a pump organ, and we played and sang for hours. No one ever questioned that a 12 year old drove the car alone that day. Upon my safe arrival back at Aunt Laura's that evening, I quickly pulled the car into the garage and went inside for dinner. The car was never missed. With so few cars on the road in those days, it was a miracle that I wasn't spotted and pulled over by the police.

Often as Aunt Laura and Anna gathered up supplies at the farm, I went next door to watch the neighbors making fresh scrapple. The adults took turns patiently stirring the mixture with a large wooden paddle over a wood fire in the front yard. The smell of the fresh meat and corn meal bubbling away in the huge black kettle was too much to resist. I stood there patiently watching and waiting. They were generous people who always gave me a steaming bowlful, and I relished every bite.

One particularly warm afternoon was my most memorable visit to the farm. After we pulled into the dirt driveway, scattering chickens along the way, Aunt Laura slid out of the car and called out the caretaker. He was always prompt about coming over to greet us, interrupting whatever he was doing, but not today. We looked all over for him, shouting his name, but got no response. Aunt Laura searched the fields and the house to no avail, and finally went into the barn. I was at her side as we entered the barn and found him. He was hanging from one of the rafters with a rope knotted tightly around his neck, his face devoid of color.

In spite of my own circumstances, I felt pity for this man. I wondered what could possess a man to end his own life. Standing there in my worn out knickers, staring at the ashen form hanging limply from the rafter, my thoughts went rapidly from pity to hope as the thought occurred to me that he wouldn't be needing those trousers any more.

In her usual business-like manner, Aunt Laura whisked me outside to play while she sent for the undertaker. Nothing ever seemed to rattle Aunt Laura, not even this pathetic suicide. It seemed more of an inconvenience to her than anything else.

A few days later while we were cleaning out the caretaker's house, Aunt Laura presented me with some new trousers. They were really old trousers but seemed like brand new to me. I had always worn knickers, so this was a big day for me, my first pair of long pants. After a few tucks and an alteration or two, I felt like a king in my new long pants, and it didn't matter one bit to me that they had once belonged to a man we found hanging in the barn.

4
Grandfather Wells

My grandfather, John Wells, was a Civil War veteran. He joined the Army in July of 1864, when he was 18 years old, and served with the 196th Infantry Regiment of Pennsylvania Volunteers, Company I. Upon completion of his term, he re-enlisted and served with the 192nd Regiment of Pennsylvania Volunteers, Company F. His second term took him to Virginia, where he was mustered out at Harper's Ferry in August of 1865. He told me, "We were discharged right where we were and walked home from there. I wasn't sure which way to go."

My grandfather was English, and a year after the war ended he married Mary Elizabeth Shunk, a Native American, born in 1849. Together they had eight children, one of whom was Harry, my father, who was born in 1872. The others were Sarah, Katie, Elizabeth, Franklin, John, Emma, and Laura, the aunt with whom I was presently living. My father told us that Grandfather met his bride during his walk back home from the Civil War. They eventually married and even though my grandmother was ostracized because of her heritage, my father often spoke with great pride of his Native American mother.

My grandmother's father, Peter Shunk, was born in 1826 and fought in the Civil War when he was thirty-eight years old. He was a canal boater and shoemaker who enlisted in the Army in August of 1864 and served in Company G of the 198th Regiment of Pennsylvania Volunteers. He was wounded in the right leg when a musket ball went clear through his ankle while fighting at Lewis Farm Virginia and was mustered out in June of 1865. Sometime after the war he became an engineer and married Sarah Ann Edwards, a young lady who was born in Wales in 1830. Mary Elizabeth Shunk was their first child; their second child was born just 6 months later. We are certain that Mary Elizabeth was either 'taken in' or adopted by the Shunks, as she was Native American and they were Welsh.

It is interesting to note that two generations of my family, my Grandfather Wells and his father-in-law (my Great-Grandfather Shunk) fought in the Civil War at the same time.

In his later years, my grandfather lived with his daughter, my Aunt Laura, in a room on the second floor of her boardinghouse. During my stay with Aunt Laura, I'd often go upstairs and visit him in his room. He called me Bobby, and I called him Grandpop. He looked a lot like me, and I was proud of him because he had been a soldier. He had earned a few medals in the Civil War and displayed them proudly on the dresser in his room. He was quite old, in his nineties, and was missing one eye. I never asked him about the eye he kept closed all the time, I was afraid he might show it to me. My father told me Grandfather lost his eye in the war. That might explain why his first hitch was cut short and why he re-enlisted after a five month hiatus.

I enjoyed talking with him because I loved hearing stories about Abraham Lincoln and the Civil War. One of his proudest memories was meeting and shaking the hand of Abraham Lincoln in Gettysburg, Pennsylvania on November 19, 1863, when Lincoln delivered his famous address. Grandfather was just 17 years old at the time. He spoke warmly of his love for the President and reminded me often of his hatred of Rebels.

He loathed slavery even more than Rebels and shared a story about a young slave he encountered on his walk north from Harper's Ferry. The lad was very young and had recently gained his freedom. He was alone and wandering about when Grandfather encountered him walking along the road. In making his acquaintance, Grandfather found that the boy had no last name. He had been a slave since birth. They spoke at length as they journeyed together toward home when the boy said to Grandfather that 'Wells' was a fine name and wondered if he might be permitted to take it as his own. Grandfather graciously gave the lad his approval. Thus began a whole new branch of the Wells family.

Another story, one that always made him chuckle, was about trading coffee for tobacco. The Yanks always had ample supplies of coffee, and the Rebels had plenty of hard tack tobacco. Occasionally during a scrimmage, Grandfather said, "a Rebel soldier would holler over to us, 'you got any coffee?' And we would yell back, 'yea, we got coffee, you got any tobacco?' The Rebels would yell 'yea, we got tobacco, let's trade.'" One man from each side would meet halfway, exchange the coffee and tobacco, go back to his line, and the fighting resumed. My grandfather got a kick out of that. "We already made coffee out of those grounds!" he said.

The many fascinating hours I spent with my grandfather kindled in me a desire to become a soldier. I imagined how courageous he must have been because he volunteered to go to war. He loved his country so much that he freely chose to fight, never giving a thought to the dangers involved. I was in awe of his courage and patriotism and decided that I wanted to grow up to be just like him.

His shoulder bore a tattoo of a fireman's ladder. Missing from the picture was the other half, a fireman's hook that should have crossed over the ladder. The hook and ladder was the traditional symbol of a firefighter or fire station. My grandfather was proud of the fact that he had been a volunteer fireman in the City of Reading for many years. The tattoo was incomplete because he was "called out to fight a fire during the procedure," he said, and never returned to have it finished.

He carried a cane and thumped it hard on the floor whenever he needed anything. Aunt Laura would hurry up the stairs and tend to his needs. He loved whiskey, and she allowed him a small glass each day with a bit of sugar. What she didn't know was that he had bottles of whiskey hidden in his mattress. He had cut holes in the fabric and shoved the bottles down into the stuffing in order to hide them from her. I don't know who supplied him with whiskey, but I never told Aunt Laura about his secret.

Grandfather died six weeks shy of his 96th birthday. He choked to death on chewing tobacco. His death certificate stated myocardial changes, but we knew the truth. He loved tobacco and chewed it twenty-four hours a day, even while he slept. Sometimes I'd go into his room while he was sleeping just to see his jaws moving. I had grown quite fond of him, especially since he was a soldier.

Because he was a Civil War veteran, and one of the oldest surviving vets in Berks County, he was honored on numerous occasions by serving as Marshall in Memorial Day and Veterans' Day parades in downtown Reading, and once in Washington D.C. I was fond of my grandfather and will always cherish the memories I have of the times I spent with him.

5
My Father

While I was living with Aunt Laura, I learned to play a few chords on the guitar from some of my buddies in the neighborhood. I'd strum and sing *The Boardinghouse* to Aunt Laura. It was a nasty song, and she hated it. She would chase me outside with her broom every time I sang it, and if she caught me, I'd spend the next several hours locked in the cellar. She rarely caught me, but I do remember the sting of her broom and serving some time in that musty dark room below the kitchen. I loved getting a rise out of her. Eventually I became quite a handful, so she sent me to Fritztown to stay with my father for the remainder of the summer.

The stay with my dad wasn't a pleasant one because we didn't get along. We were both bullheaded and quick-tempered, and it was difficult for me to obey someone I hardly knew. My dad was 63 years old at the time, a difficult age in one's life to begin rearing a child, and a difficult child at that. But it wasn't always bad; in fact there were a few perks. Dad could bake. He couldn't cook to save his soul, but he baked the best sugar cookies in town. My dad also loved to fish and so did I, so he took my brother, John, and me with him often. The fish we caught always ended up in the frying pan, and he occasionally brought home a snapper turtle for soup.

He took us hunting with him often. We trapped muskrats for their meat and hides and hunted groundhogs with shotguns. After some practice I actually hit a few, but soon realized that I didn't like shooting animals. My dad cooked everything we shot. Everything! At night he took us hunting for raccoons, but killing animals wasn't fun anymore. I wanted nothing more to do with hunting, and I'd had quite enough 'coon stew. By now I was really missing Aunt Laura's cooking. My dad raised his own chickens, so we occasionally had a familiar meal, but I'll never be able rid myself of the mental picture of him twisting the head off a chicken in one swift motion with his bare hands.

My brother, Johnny, had been living with my father since our parents split up. I believe my father took Johnny when he was a baby against my mother's wishes, and would probably have taken me as well had I not been in the hospital. My sister, Betty, was left behind with my mother, as well as the children from her first marriage. Johnny never saw our mother again and sadly never even knew what she looked like.

Being with Johnny again was good for the both of us. We looked very much alike and got along quite well. Together we walked a couple of miles to Galen Hall Golf course where we queued up in the caddy house hoping to earn some cash. After all the regular caddies went out with their clients, we waited around hopefully for a client or two of our own. We often got one, and for the thirty-five cent salary we earned we had the privilege of walking the entire 18-hole golf course lugging a heavy golf bag on a hot summer day. Afterwards Johnny and I hiked all the way back to our dad's house and turned the money over to him.

Because I didn't know my father very well, I didn't obey him. I resented his ordering me about. One morning after an argument, he looked me squarely in the eyes and in a threatening tone of voice said, "Pack your rags and get out." Because I was confused and frightened, I got out quickly; he was very angry and meant business. I had been shuffled around my whole short life, never feeling like I belonged anywhere, and now my own father was kicking me out. Even though I didn't get along with my dad, I was happy living there with Johnny. He and I had grown close.

As fate would have it, I was to be sent back to Aunt Laura at the boardinghouse, but instead I headed for the hills, at least the steep hill behind my dad's house. A half mile or so from my dad's place, on the top of a wooded slope, sat a musty old cabin. I didn't want to go back to Aunt Laura; I felt unwanted there, so for the next several weeks I took up residence in the old log cabin.

The cabin was filthy and missing part of the roof, but still managed to stand on its own. It was a palace to me, peaceful and quiet, nobody telling me what to do. Johnny sneaked food up to me whenever he could, but not very much of it, so I was good and hungry for the next couple of weeks. I missed Aunt Laura's chili, but not enough to make me go back there. So I subsisted on the occasional bowl of stew Johnny brought me when my father wasn't around. The stew was always the same, alphabets with a few random pieces of meat, turnips, carrots, and potatoes, but I ate it anyway because I was hungry.

By day I explored the woods, and then returned to the cabin each night to sleep. Although I resided here only briefly, the sights and sounds of the woods surrounding me restored my sense of normality. Eventually, the nights became cool and uncomfortable, and I feared repercussions by my father against Johnny if he got caught bringing me food, so I made the decision to go back and stay with Aunt Laura.

Soon after I returned to the boardinghouse, I was told that my mother had passed away. Her death certificate stated that she died from dropsy (congestive heart failure); she was 47 years old. I was just 13 at the time but vividly remember my last visit to her bedside at the hospital a few weeks before she died. One of her legs was grossly swollen and she looked old to me, but I remember thinking she was pretty. She motioned for me to sit with her on the bed, and I did. She was very ill and knew she was going to die as she softly said to me, "Bobby, when I die, don't you cry." I promised her that I wouldn't, and on the day of her funeral, sitting tall in my seat at the funeral parlor, listening to the country music being played in her memory, I kept my promise.

To this day, I have vivid memories of standing by her freshly dug grave, gazing into its depths as her crude wooden casket was lowered directly into the earth. There was no fanfare, not even a marker; she was too poor. I felt no remorse at my loss because she was pretty much a stranger to me; yet I knew that I'd lost something important in my life, but wouldn't come to understand completely what I'd lost until many years later.

6
My Education

My first experience with school happened a few months after I came home from the hospital. I was ten years old and completely illiterate. In the 1930s hospitals did not provide their patients with an education, so my mother enrolled me in Tyson Schoener Elementary School, in Reading, in September. I hated school from that first day. It was too regimented, consumed too many hours of my time, and I wasn't used to taking orders from anyone.

In spite of the fact that I was ten years old, I was put into first grade. I was so big, the kids thought I was the teacher! Needless to say, this was not a pleasant experience for me. I had a great sense of adventure and couldn't see the world from my seat in a first-grade classroom. Thus I became bothersome and, to say the least, a troublemaker. Within a short period of time, my first grade teacher decided she wanted me removed from her class. First graders didn't usually smoke, curse at their teacher, and play hooky from school. Because of my indifference toward school, I made very little progress even though I remained in first grade until the end of the school year. It was hell for me and summer vacation was a welcome relief.

My handicap proved a great disadvantage for me with the kids at school. To say that they were cruel was quite an understatement. The brace I wore on my leg for almost a year since leaving the hospital gave them license to harass and mock me. Sometimes they threw stones at me. However, my only friend, Tony Borsalino, took care of the problem. Tony was a big, awkward kid who was ostracized by his peers. In spite of Tony's flaws, his sheer size frightened everyone, but not me. Tony and I had something in common; nobody liked either one of us, but we got along just fine. Tony took me under his wing and beat the stuffing out of any kid who doubted the seriousness of his loyalty to me. The taunting soon stopped and the brace eventually came off, but my friendship with Tony lasted many years.

By some miracle, I survived my first year in school, and even though I had made very little progress, I was rewarded with a promotion to fourth grade the following year. I was actually a very bright kid with a bad attitude brought on by the manner in which I was mistreated by teachers. I had come to believe that all teachers were cruel, and I had never been treated cruelly before.

School was stifling to my creativity, curiosity and wanderlust, so I resisted. Still unable read or write or do simple arithmetic by age eleven, I was left to wallow. Living mostly inside my head while confined within those walls, I dreamed of great adventures that awaited me as I imagined cowboys and horses, and faraway places.

School was not completely worthless, however; I enjoyed art class and the art instructor. I often wondered if she really was a teacher because she was kind to me. I also enjoyed singing, and might have enjoyed music class if it hadn't involved so much hair pulling.

My music teacher had developed her own unique method for getting us to sing on pitch. She'd blow into that damned pitch pipe while pulling our hair straight up if she wanted us to sing higher or straight down if we were supposed to sing lower. She could have pulled my hair all day and it would not have made any difference to me. I hated music class and that miserable woman.

Physical education was my favorite class, not for the exercise it involved, or the fresh air I'd breathe, but for the opportunities it provided me. Gym class was usually conducted outdoors in the school yard, thus giving me ample opportunities to sprint from the school property in the middle of the day. I sometimes didn't return to school for a few days, thus earning the opportunity to become acquainted with the school district's truant officer.

Fourth grade was just more of the same. I still wasn't learning, but took advantage of every opportunity to get myself into trouble. By mid-year I was moved to the sixth grade and put into a 'special' class, mainly because I was too difficult to handle. I soon found out that I was in the 'dummy class' as it was publicly referred to, and nobody, students or teachers, let me forget it.

My sixth grade homeroom teacher was cruel. She was more a warden than a teacher and called us dummies and threatened us. I was hardened by now, but I felt a great deal of sympathy for some of the kids. The class was a mix of kids with physical handicaps, learning difficulties, speech defects and behavior problems. Anyone who made progress with his studies and never spoke back was exempted. The rest of us were thrown into this 'dummy class.'

The teacher was most cruel to the kids with speech defects. She called them 'dumb' and made them cry. I'll never forget a pretty girl in my class who had slurred speech and had a great deal of difficulty speaking. The teacher was merciless to her and always made her cry. I remember feeling great sadness for the girl and anger towards the teacher. I sassed that miserable woman every opportunity I got, pretty much on a regular basis, and she punished me by keeping me after school often so I would miss the bus and have to walk home. I lived more than a mile from school and still wore a brace on my leg.

She carried a pointed stick and hit us with it anytime we didn't know the answer to a question. Needless to say, she hit me a lot. She usually struck us across the back or hands, and sometimes on the upper arms. She knew where it hurt. She checked my fingers daily for cigarette stains, which were ever present. The stains were hard to remove, so I suffered her abuse because I smoked. I'd get really angry and tell her to "go to hell," and then she'd fly into a rage and hit me again. Often, out of desperation, I'd sprint right out of the building and wouldn't return to school for a day or two. Her sister was the truant officer for the school district, and I remember being terrified of her each time she showed up at the house to round me up. She was nasty, too; I guess the temperament ran in the family.

One afternoon, a local radio station invited our class to sing a song on the radio. I was living with Aunt Margaret by now; my mother had passed away. My aunt was very excited for me and promised to listen to the radio that afternoon. At the radio station when we were just about to sing, my miserable music teacher looked directly at me, put a finger to her lips, and told me to "be quiet." She did not want me to sing. The rest of the class sang, and then we all went home.

That afternoon when I arrived home from school, Aunt Margaret looked at me, smiled and said, "Bobby, I heard you sing, and you were really good!" She continued to say that she could hear me above the others. She was very proud of me. I never told her what happened, or that I didn't sing at all that afternoon at the radio station. I didn't have the heart to tell her. She was a thoughtful woman who treated me well, and I will never forget her kindness.

I have only one fond memory of school that remains very clear to me to this day. I loved Viking ships and I remember making one in art class. We cut the ship out of colored paper and pasted it onto the cover of a notebook that we made. I was proud of that Viking ship and managed to keep it my whole life. How ironic that I should later become part of a Viking Battalion in the U.S. Army.

7
Aunt Margaret

Immediately after my mother's death, Children's Aid stepped in and sent me to live with my mother's sister, Margaret Roland Hoffman, on Little Hampden Boulevard. My sister, Betty, went to live with our older, now married half-sister, Catharine, and my younger brother, John, was already living with our father. He had been with my father since my parents' separation.

Right from the start I felt welcome in Aunt Margaret's modest home, unlike Aunt Laura's boardinghouse where I felt like a servant. Her dark hair, which she wore curled into a bun on the back of her head, reminded me of my mother. She was kind and gentle like my mother, as well, having little effect or control over me or my sense of wanderlust. Though her own two boys, Johnny and Albert, rarely disobeyed her, she was always tolerant of my disobedience and dealt with me fairly. Even though I quickly grew fond of Aunt Margaret, I was well aware of the fact that the family was poor and felt as though I was taking from them. I had never learned how to be part of a family, only how to be alone, and these feelings would eventually cause me to set out on my own.

Soon after I came to live with Aunt Margaret, I became smitten with a girl named Rosemary. She played tennis in City

Park with her girl friends, and I would sneak up to watch her. However, Aunt Margaret found out about this because my cousins Albert and Johnny told her. So she took me aside one day and firmly told me, "Bobby, if you get this girl pregnant, you'd better be prepared to marry her!" "Pregnant!" I shrieked, "We haven't even smooched yet!" I just liked being around her, and she liked me too. She used to take me home with her; she had a mother and one sister, and they would invite me to stay for dinner. They were very nice to me, in spite of the fact that I was poor and could never take Rosemary anywhere.

Life with Aunt Margaret was good. She fed me well and treated me like I was one of her own boys, the same two boys who told her about Rosemary and me. My smoking drove her crazy, but there was nothing she could do to stop me. She would regularly check my fingers to see if they were yellow, and they usually were; then I'd catch a gentle scolding. She really cared about me, but as hard as she tried, had little control over me. I was always running off looking for new adventures.

The only thing that disturbed me about Aunt Margaret was that she seemed overly concerned about the bowel habits of her children, me included. She said to me every day, "Bobby, did you have a BM today?" My reply was always the same, whether or not I had had a BM, until one day when I didn't have a BM. Instead, I was in an awful lot of pain, enough to make me admit it. So Aunt Margaret gave me a laxative, thinking I was constipated. The pain only got worse so she called Dr. Tucker-Greene, who came straight to our house. The doctor immediately sent me to the city hospital where I was diagnosed with a ruptured appendix and underwent immediate emergency surgery.

I survived the surgery but remained unconscious for most of the next week, and finally went home after ten days. This was very major surgery in 1936, and it was really a miracle that I survived. Speaking of miracles, I had an unforgettable experience during my surgery. I believe I 'passed on' briefly during the procedure, because I vividly remember leaving my body and being able to see my surroundings for a few moments. The episode was brief but astounding, and then suddenly I came back. I never talked about my near-death experience until many years later when I became an adult, but remember it clearly to this day. Aunt Margaret nursed me back to health that summer, doting over me like a mother hen. Her feelings for me were palpable; only my mother had treated me as well.

While I lived with Aunt Margaret, I worked for the milkman for an entire winter. I loved that job mostly because I loved the milkman's horse. Joe was a beautiful big black and white horse who watched for me each morning. Aunt Margaret woke me promptly at 3:00 A.M. each day, and I quickly dressed and ran down the block in the dark to meet the milkman on 12th Street. Joe stood there patiently in the middle of the street looking in my direction and was always happy to see me. I remember how he struggled to climb up the steep hills on ice and snow in his special shoes. The milk truck was heavy, but he was a strong horse and always managed to get the job done.

Joe belonged to the St. Lawrence Dairy and was well cared for. He was loved by everyone, especially by me. When Joe was off duty, he spent his leisure time in a stable at 10th & Bingaman Streets where I often visited him on the weekends. Before leaving I'd throw my arms around his huge neck and press my face into his warm fur. There is nothing quite as wonderful as the smell of a horse. After spending time with Joe, I'd stop at 9th and Bingaman Streets and spend several minutes gazing into the front window of the dairy. It was entertaining to watch milk being poured into bottles as they passed by the front window of the dairy.

My job involved carrying bottles of milk and cream and setting them down on the customers' porches. When we were halfway down the block, the milkman whistled and Joe, with ears pricked, would pull the milk wagon down the street to meet us. Then we lifted more milk bottles from the wagon and started all over again. Joe was a smart horse. We finished our milk deliveries by 5:30 or 6:00 A.M. and I went back home for breakfast before going to school. I earned one dollar per week, as much milk as I could drink, and the love of a fine horse helping the milkman that winter.

8
My Buddies

I started smoking when I was eleven years old. I bought little packs of Bull Durham for about six cents a pack and rolled my own. My mother occasionally gave me a little money when she had some, but she didn't know that I used it to buy cigarettes. She was not a smoker and didn't suspect that I was. Watching people smoke fascinated me, and one day I said to myself, "I want to blow a little smoke around, too." That's how I got started. My friends, mostly kids from the neighborhood, and I thought we were really tricky because we could blow smoke out of our noses. If you could do that, you were a real smoker! Sometimes when we had no money for cigarettes, we'd roll dried silk from ears of field corn and smoke that.

Sonny was one of my best buddies. I met him shortly after I was released from the tuberculosis sanitarium in Berks County. It wasn't very long before I was running the streets, and I soon had a bunch of good friends. Here in the city, there were lots of kids to get into mischief with. Sonny was the nephew of Martha and John Erb. They lived very close to us, just around the corner, in fact. Sonny and I became good friends. He was living with his aunt and uncle because his father was in prison. I never knew why he was in prison, but he was there for a long time.

I soon grew very fond of Sonny's Aunt Martha and Uncle John. Sonny had a real home with them. They became pretty fond of me, too, and before long started treating me like a son. They were good people who loved kids but were never able to have any of their own. Martha often invited me and Betty in for a meal.

Martha took in a young lady named Anne Swink, who was orphaned at a very young age when her parents were killed in an accident. She had a permanent home with Martha and helped out with the household chores and cooking. Anne was a kind woman who took an interest in my education. I remember how she sat with me for hours patiently trying to teach me how to read and write. Anne and I developed a friendship that lasted until she passed away a few years ago, well into her eighties.

Martha came to know my mother and regularly bought groceries to help her out. When my mother died, Martha and John tried to adopt me. Because they were not blood relatives, their efforts were futile. I was greatly disappointed and was sent to live with my mother's sister, Margaret. I had already become a part of Martha's family, and that connection would last a lifetime.

We kids were mischievous, to say the least. Sonny and I went down Chestnut Street, over the railroad tracks, and played in the coal piles. Coal was brought in and dropped there by railroad cars, and coal dealers came in, loaded up their trucks and delivered it to homeowners. We jumped and played in the coal piles until we were completely blackened, and then we went home. I was well aware of the consequence of playing in the coal piles; Aunt Margaret would toss me directly into a tub of warm water. I wasn't too fond of water back then, especially bath water, but the exhilaration of jumping in the coal far outweighed the brief humiliation of the tub.

We kids were very curious about birds and insects, and bird anatomy was of special interest. We occasionally caught a bird, usually a robin, and 'sawed it apart' with the rusty little hacksaw I found in the shed. We were playing doctor, I guess, dissecting them and looking for their hearts. We soon learned that there were other things in there as well, slimy things that smelled a little funny. We cared about the birds enough to kill them first by twisting their necks so they wouldn't feel any pain when we later dissected them.

Our self-education in science involved light, specifically the light on the butt end of a firefly. We called them lightening bugs right up to the point where we physically removed their light by twisting it off, and saving it in a jar until we had a whole jarful. Unfortunately, the lights went out a short time later, lasting only slightly longer than the bugs who donated them. This was a thoroughly fascinating experiment, although short-lived, but kept us intrigued over the next couple of summers.

Sonny and I hopped freight trains just for fun. Railroad tracks ran right through the center of Reading, and approaching trains traveled very slowly through the city, so it was an easy task to run along side and climb up into the car. Whoever got on first lent a hand to the other; we took turns doing this. Then we'd ride the cars for a couple of blocks through town and leap off just as the train exited the city, before it picked up too much speed and held us hostage.

Sometimes we'd climb up on the cars and run along the top, while the train was in motion, leaping from car to car. Leaping across the cars in the direction in which they were going was the most difficult and took the greatest amount of concentration; but turning around and leaping the other direction was a cinch. It was an exhilarating experience, and we became quite skilled at it. This was a great adventure and miraculously we never fell off or got caught.

This fascination with the railroad, although a dangerous one, had its perks. We soon learned that the railroad station was a great place to find cigarette butts. Passengers would toss lit cigarettes, many of which were only half smoked, onto the ground before climbing aboard the train. We'd wait for the trains to pull out, and then help ourselves to the butts. This provided us with an unlimited supply of cigarettes.

Occasionally, Martha would give us each a dime to buy a model airplane. The kits were challenging and took up a good bit of our time till we glued the entire frame together, then pasted the paper over the plane. The planes were somewhat small and flew by turning the propeller with a finger, thus twisting tightly the attached rubber band. In one swift motion, we released our finger from the propeller and hurled the plane forward into the air at the same time. After a short while, we became bored with flying them, so we'd go down to the railroad, climb up on top of a freight car, set the planes on fire, and let 'em rip. That was exciting!!! The only downside was we'd have to go back to Martha for another dime and start the whole process over again.

I once stole a bag of marbles from the five & ten cent store at 6th and Penn Streets. This was the first time I ever stole anything, and I didn't get caught. I entered the store, slipped the small bag of marbles into my coat pocket, and then slipped out the back door which was adjacent to the toy department. I knew it was wrong to steal, but my cousins, Johnny and Albert, wanted me to play marbles, and I didn't have any marbles. The little bit of money I got my hands on bought my Bull Durham. Johnny and Albert didn't smoke, so they didn't understand. Now that I had my own marbles I was finally able to play, but eventually I lost them all anyway because I wasn't very good at the game.

Even at my young age, I knew that stealing was wrong. I felt bad about stealing the marbles, and I never did it again. However, when I was a runaway, I occasionally stole food or milk. Hunger was a powerful incentive, but I regretted it all the same.

Johnny, Albert and I spent a lot of time fishing. We'd walk more than two miles from our house on Little Hampden Boulevard to Bernhart's Dam. First we'd spend an hour or so digging for earthworms for bait, then head over to the water's edge for some serious fishing. Aunt Margaret never seemed to mind when we arrived home hours later with a stringer full of sunfish, and an occasional perch or bass. Later that evening the fish would magically appear on our dinner plates, fried to a golden brown. Aunt Margaret was a great cook, and nothing ever tasted better to us after a long day's fishing on a warm summer afternoon.

Tommy, Betty, and I went to the movies whenever we had a little money. A movie cost us a dime each. The dime was usually my cigarette money, but I just couldn't resist a good western, even if it meant going without cigarettes for a few days. I especially loved cowboy movies, and stars like Tom Mix and Hoop Gibson were my favorites. They were real tough hombres, who were always fighting with the Indians. I always sided with the Indians and especially enjoyed when a cowboy was shot with an arrow in the back and fell off his horse. I knew the hero would prevail, regardless of how many cowboys lay dying in the desert sun, and that was okay with me.

I remember being turned away once because the price went up to eleven cents and we each had only a dime. We were greatly disappointed and devised a scheme so that it wouldn't happen again. Our plan was simple—we'd sneak into the theater with a crowd. It was easy to do especially when there were a lot of families with kids, which was usually the case. We'd split up and work our way into the crowd, then go right in with the kids. It was surprisingly easy; nobody ever noticed, and we never got caught.

9

On My Own

In the spring of my 14th year, I ran away from home, slipping out of the house when Aunt Margaret was busy. I had thought about it for some time now and wanted to become a cowboy. I had seen a few cowboy movies in my time and knew this was the life for me. I went down to the train yards at 7th and Walnut and hopped a freight train headed west, and remember thinking that it wasn't so difficult; in fact, the way things were going, I'd be in 'Kansas' in no time.

The train hadn't started moving yet when I heard voices outside. I knew immediately that I was in trouble when a railroad bull reached in and grabbed me, not so gently, and dragged me roughly out of the car and down the tracks to the station. I was momentarily startled and slightly bruised, but mostly I was angry. After a brief wait at the station, a couple of police showed up and hauled me into City Hall.

They put me in a lock-up in the basement. I resisted as they grabbed me and threw me into the cell, pushing me so hard that I was thrown to the floor. I was tall for my age but thin; I don't believe I weighed 100 pounds. The next morning I was photographed and fingerprinted, then put into a vehicle. I had no idea where they were taking me.

A few hours later, I had a new home in Berks County Prison—thirty days for hopping a freight train. I told them my name was Smith, Robert Smith, no address. They never questioned it; they just threw me, a 14 year old boy, into prison. After a couple of days I settled in, I really didn't mind it too much. I had my own cell, was allowed to exercise in the yard, and people left me alone. The food was good, and I stayed out of trouble by weaving rag rugs earning just enough money to buy some Bull Durham. In spite of the fact that I was incarcerated, time passed quickly, and the free time I had was spent in planning my next attempt at becoming a cowboy.

Aunt Margaret never new of my whereabouts or that I had been in jail, and that suited me fine. But I wonder now, as a parent, what she must have thought. I am sure she was worried sick by my disappearance, but that thought never occurred to me at the time. I felt as though I was a burden to her and was doing her a favor by leaving. Her husband, John, was not well, working at odd jobs to support the family, and I felt as though I was taking from them, even though she treated me as well as her own boys. I also felt as though I was destined to go.

Thirty days later, I was released from jail and delivered to the Hope Rescue Mission in downtown Reading. That was a stroke of luck for me. The guys there knew how to hop a freight train without getting caught, and they were happy to educate anyone who dropped in, including me. I stayed a few days, had a few more meals, and then set out on my own.

Before I left Reading on my second attempt to go west, I took up residence under the Buttonwood Street Bridge. My time alone under the bridge was peaceful; nobody bothered me.

I was very resourceful and figured out quickly how to get food, shelter for the night, and most importantly, how to avoid the police. Early each morning, before daybreak, I sneaked out and helped myself to fresh-baked buns and milk off nearby porches. I always returned to my home under the bridge to enjoy my breakfast. This routine became my ritual every morning for about a week, alternating houses in a two-block area.

The nights were a little cool and I didn't have a jacket, so I cuddled up against the bridge abutment wrapped in newspaper, and fell asleep. My stay here lasted about a week until the urge to go west hit me again. No one ever bothered me or knew I was here, except the pigeons. They sat calmly, side by side, and made strange cooing sounds, keeping a watchful eye on me.

By now I was pretty confident that I could catch a freight train without getting caught, and on my first attempt, which was made after dark, I was on my way.

It was cold in the freight train that night, and I didn't have anything warm to put on, so I tore some of the heavy insulating paper from the wall of the car and used it for a cover. In fact, it hadn't occurred to me to pack anything at all. That would have meant a trip back to Aunt Margaret's, and I didn't want to go back there. I was resourceful and tough and didn't need anything to survive. I was better off alone. I believe it was this experience, living on the road, outside in the cold, with little to eat, for many months that prepared me for my future as an infantry soldier.

There were a couple of bums huddled in the corners of the car I was riding, but I stayed clear of them. I didn't bother them, and fortunately they left me alone. I wasn't planning on getting mixed up with any riffraff. I was on my own now and wanted to be left alone. Soon my paper cover warmed me and the rhythmic motion of the train rocked me until I was peacefully sound asleep. The morning arrived earlier than usual as I was abruptly awakened by shouting and screeching brakes just before sunrise. We had arrived already. I was in Kansas!

I peeked out of the boxcar to see what was happening. We had pulled into the yard, and the bulls were out. I was not going to be caught again, so I leapt out of the car and ran like hell straight into town. A bull spotted me, but I had the advantage of youth and he soon gave up his pursuit. A quick glance at the buildings told me something was not right. This was not Kansas; I was in Philadelphia! I had hopped the right train, but in the wrong direction.

My time alone on the streets had taught me a lot. I knew that I'd gotten off the train on the wrong side of the tracks; this was a bad section of town, so I picked up my pace and hoofed it out of there. After roaming the streets for awhile, I soon found a flop house and was able to have a meal, and for the price of a prayer, a bed for the night as well. The next morning, well rested, I made a decision to see the ocean since I was already this far east, so I hitchhiked to Asbury Park and slept in the dune grass that night.

One learns quickly to be cautious and diligent when traveling alone. I was careful to avoid the police and was constantly on the lookout for a meal. Finding shelter was always foremost in my mind. Almost every town had a mission that provided the homeless with a meal and a bed, but I didn't spend much time in towns. Therefore I didn't eat often enough and was always hungry. Bakeries handed me day old buns, and meat markets were a good source of boloney ends. When I got desperate, I'd knock on the back door of a house and tell the owner that I was willing to work for a meal. No one ever turned me away. Usually the food was brought outside, and I ate on the back porch. Sometimes I was taken into the kitchen and fed at the kitchen table.

I met a lot of kind people, many of whom not only fed me, but sent along extra food in a paper bag. And I was never asked to work or do chores, even though I always extended the offer. There were a lot of young people who were hungry, jobless or homeless during the depression years, and right now I was one of them. My time alone on the road taught me an important lesson about caring for others, especially those less fortunate.

There weren't a lot of cars on the roads in 1937, but because I traveled a lot by night, they were easy to spot by their headlights. On my way back to Philadelphia I was arrested again, this time for hitchhiking. That evening I was standing along the road, illuminated by a gas station, in hopes of being seen by an oncoming car. This way I had a better chance of getting a ride.

I soon learned that the gas station was closing down for the night. As the owner counted his money, he spotted me on the opposite side of the road, suspected that I was a troublemaker and immediately called the police. The police arrived quickly, picked me up and arrested me for hitchhiking and loitering. I was taken to police headquarters and locked in a cell for the night. The next day I was sentenced to thirty days in May's Landing County Jail in New Jersey.

I was put into a cell with three other guys, and they were a rough bunch. One of them decided he didn't like me so he mocked me and cursed at me. I wasn't very big in stature at that point in my life, but I had a big attitude, so, pissed off, I hit him hard and knocked him out.

The cops took me out of the cell immediately, roughed me up and put me in a small cell by myself—solitary confinement, with only a straw-stuffed mattress on the floor, a filthy toilet, and nothing else. After that I subsisted on a slice of bread and a cup of water two times a day for the remainder of my sentence. I was only 14 years old.

After serving 30 days, they released me and told me to "get the hell out of New Jersey, and don't come back!" I started to hitchhike my way back to Philadelphia when I was picked up by another cop. He radioed in and learned that I had just been released, so he drove me to the bridge and dropped me off. When I got out of the car he said, "Get your goddamned ass out of this state and don't you ever come back!" "Don't worry," I said, "I won't!"

* * * * *

I must confess that I never kept my word; I've been to Jersey since!

10
Liberal, Kansas

After hitchhiking my way back to Philadelphia, I managed to catch a freight train traveling west; its destination was Chicago, via Harrisburg, Pennsylvania. I hopped off the train in Harrisburg and hitchhiked from there. Each time a car stopped and asked where I was headed, I always said, "I'm going west." If the driver was headed west, he almost always picked me up. There weren't many cars in those days, but most people were kind and offered to help me.

I decided to take a break from traveling and spent a couple of nights in a flop house (a mission) in Indianapolis. They made me say prayers for my meals and bunk. When I was hungry and tired, I could become Mr. Gospel real quick. Praying comes easy when one is desperate.

Rested and fed, I set out on the road again, still headed west. Unless I was hitchhiking, before dark each day I'd look for a place to spend the night. I slept under bridges, behind signs, on the ground, and only occasionally in a mission.

I also did a lot of walking on that trip, mostly along the railroad tracks. I felt a strange sense of peace walking the tracks, and no one bothered me out there. Except for an occasional passing train and the sounds of birds, my journey along the tracks was generally quiet. Some of my most memorable moments of being alone were the times I'd sit down on the track, roll a cigarette and light it. I'd put it to my lips and draw the smoke slowly into my lungs, then exhale just as slowly through my nose. This was the life for me. After tossing the butt aside, I'd continue my journey west by following the setting sun.

On the Missouri side of the Mississippi river I did some fishing with a hand line. I improvised a fishhook from a safety pin by straightening out the pin and curling the pointed end into the shape of a hook. Next I tied a string to the top of the pin snuggly around the head. This system was especially effective with a freshly dug earthworm wriggling on the hook in a vain struggle for its life. I remember catching catfish, garfish and others; they looked big to me, probably because I was so young.

I never ate any of the fish I caught. Cooking them would have required a campfire, and I rarely built a fire. A campfire would have drawn attention to me, and I wanted none of that, so I just tossed the fish back into the water with a splash. Fishing relaxed me and provided me with some fine entertainment. Camping out by the river under the stars was peaceful, as long as I stayed clear of boats and people. The nights were cool so I stayed warm by covering up with newspaper or cardboard. Wrapped in a cocoon of newspaper warmed my tired body and lulled me into a blissful sleep.

I crossed the Missouri River on foot via a bridge from Kansas City, Missouri, to Kansas City, Kansas, just on the other side. There was a passenger railroad station there, so I waited until the train pulled out and jumped onto the steps outside the door and rode 'in style' holding on for dear life all the way to Liberal. It was a long, scenic ride, and didn't cost me a dime. This was known as 'riding the blinds' because I was in a blind spot when viewed from inside the car and could not be seen.

As the train approached Liberal, I jumped off well before it pulled into the station. Directly across the tracks from where I hopped off the train was a 'bum's jungle,' a group of homeless men who congregated together, cooked and shared food and stories. They were preparing a meal, and finding comfort in each other's company. I had learned from experience that bums always shared their food, regardless of how little they had. And today was no exception. I was hungry and went over to them, and they immediately gave me something to eat.

I had been on the road for weeks now and was tired, so I decided to hang around town for awhile, exploring whatever I could find. The local Salvation Army fixed me up with a clean set of used clothing and shoes, but first I was given a bath! The only time I begged was when I needed a little money for cigarettes, but I always offered to work for food. People here in Liberal were generous and often gave me twenty-five cents and occasionally fifty cents. I think they felt sorry for me because I was just a kid, and a homeless one at that.

The Sheriff of Liberal was a kind, round, middle-aged man who let me sleep in an empty jail cell at night. For the next few weeks I slept on a comfortable bed with a mattress and blanket. "Come and go as you please," he told me. He was sympathetic to everyone, unlike the cops in New Jersey!

My travels had taken me far; I was less than fifty miles from the Texas panhandle, almost west, soon a cowboy. However, I had been on the lam for a long time and surviving on the road alone was becoming a burden. I was weary and longed for a familiar face. The emptiness I felt lately was more than hunger, I was lonely. After spending a few weeks in Liberal, I became homesick for Betty and decided to go back. I wrote her first and asked for some money to come home. She sent me a dollar in care of the Sheriff of Liberal, and I headed home. My cowboy days were over; in fact, I hadn't even seen a single cowboy.

Over the next several weeks I retraced my steps home by hitchhiking and hopping freight trains. I was feeling very lonely at this point; I missed Betty, and I was hungry. Fortunately, my journey home went smoothly. I had been on the road for six months.

When I arrived in Reading, I could hardly wait to see my sister. I didn't want to see her at Catharine's house because Catharine would probably turn me over Children's Aid. So I went into Reading to a church where Betty was taking lessons to become a Catholic. When I arrived and asked for her, I was told she was 'right inside.' Betty was a sight for sore eyes and smiled as she threw her arms around me.

She took me home immediately to get me something to eat. When we arrived at Catharine's house, she hid me in the alley, told Catharine I was back, and asked her for some food. Catharine agreed to feed me but not in the house. "Feed him out back," she said.

By Catherine's standards, I was unfit to enter the house. Weeks had passed since my bath in Liberal and I was filthy, but Betty didn't seem to notice; she was too delighted to have me back. Catharine had an infant son at the time and didn't want him exposed to germs, so Betty brought the food out to the yard, and we sat together while I ate. She called her fiancé, Jack, and he picked me up a few hours later and took me to Aunt Laura's boardinghouse. Any thoughts I had of running away from Aunt Laura vanished the moment I walked into her house and sat down to a bowl of her chili. I agreed to move back into my small room on the second floor of the boardinghouse and help out by doing dishes, wiping tables and staying out of trouble.

In the meantime Aunt Margaret, my legal guardian, was making plans for me. She decided that I would join the Civilian Conservation Corps. I wasn't quite old enough to join, so she lied and told them I was sixteen, even though I had just turned fifteen. Told that I would be going cross country to Idaho by train, as a paying passenger this time, to become a lumberjack, was a dream come true for me. Aunt Margaret's decision was a wise one and would set in motion events that would change my life, not just for the better, but forever.

* * * * *

I didn't learn until many years later just how much my sister, Betty, worried about me when I was a runaway, hopping freight trains and traveling on my own. I never thought about how my actions affected others. I was told that she never turned away a single hungry soul who ever showed up at her door asking for food, in gratitude to all those kind individuals who made sure that I never went hungry when I was a kid.

11
Civilian Conservation Corps

As a result of the stock market crash of 1929 and the depression that followed, millions of people in this country were jobless. The Civilian Conservation Corps was one of several programs conceived by President Roosevelt to provide jobs for the unemployed and was specifically geared to providing employment for young men. This Corps was to be a peaceful army of civilians who would go out and help restore the environment, primarily our nation's decimated forests and national parks.

Between 1933 and 1942 the Corps planted over 3 billion trees in forests and parks all over the country. The Corps was also involved in clearing timber as well. In September, I was sent to Priest Lake in Coolin, Idaho, for a six-month hitch to become a lumberjack, producing telephone poles for shipment to the Southwest. I had just turned fifteen a month before I was shipped to Idaho by train. The train also carried a young man from Reading, Willie Weller, who would become a life-long friend and my future brother-in-law.

Lumberjacking was just the challenge I needed. My boss was a lumberjack from Montana, and one of the largest and strongest men I had ever seen. He was a big son of a bitch, kind of mean, and definitely too big to beat up, so none of us ever gave him any trouble. He put me on a two-man saw crew, one man on each end of a six-foot saw. We learned how to drop a tree exactly where we wanted it to fall, not an easy task, and these were huge trees. We made our first cut, and then two ax men would chop at it until there was a wedge in the tree. Next, we went to the opposite side of the tree, cutting with our saw until the tree fell, always falling away from us in exactly the direction we had planned.

After the tree was felled, the ax men chopped off all the branches and bark. The trees, huge evergreens, were then pulled with bull hooks to a position where they could be slid down the hill, large end first, and loaded into trucks. From there they were taken to Priest River and put into large tanks where they were soaked in a substance to preserve them.

One rule I will never forget was to yell 'Timber' when felling a tree. We were told that this was a state law and failure to do so was punished by having to work even harder, and we already worked hard enough! Never really sure about that state law, I wasn't going to take any chances. In fact, I never got into any mischief at all. 'Till I got my day's work in, I was too damned tired to cause any trouble.

Autumn in Idaho was glorious but brief, and winter arrived early that year, bringing bitter cold weather and mountains of snow. The hard work and adequate clothing kept us warm; otherwise I'm certain we'd have frozen to death.

We were given a week off midway through our six month hitch. Every day for a week we were taken to Spokane by truck for a little sightseeing. Most of the guys returned to camp each night, but a few brave souls chose to stay in Spokane for the duration. Knowing we were less than one hundred miles from the Pacific Ocean motivated me to head west. Peugeot Sound was a day and a half travel by train, so a buddy and I hopped a freight train out of Spokane that first night.

My prior experiences on the road served me well on this trip. I knew how to avoid the police, the railroad bulls, and how to get a meal. The weather was cold, but we stayed warm and comfortable in our uniforms and jackets. After our brief glimpse of the Pacific, we hitchhiked back to Spokane just in time to catch a truck for our return trip to camp. Our side trip, which remained our secret, was a scenic and pleasant adventure.

The Corps fed us, clothed us, worked us hard, and treated us well. We earned about thirty dollars a month, of which twenty-five dollars was sent home to our families. That left us with five dollars a month for ourselves, and we used it mostly for cigarettes. We were issued army type uniforms, which we wore all day long. We had all come from poor families and felt like we were someone special in our uniforms; we were part of something important now. I thought this must be what it felt like to be in the Army.

The food at camp was good, and there was plenty of it. We had a postage exchange where we could buy cigarettes, chocolate bars and postcards to send home. I did send some postcards home, but the guys had to spell out every word for me. We slept in barracks in small army-type beds that were very basic, clean and comfortable. The guys got along well, we had fun together, and I formed a life long friendship with Willie Weller. We worked hard and the days passed quickly.

After dark we'd lie in our cots and listen to the wolves all around us. They were howling, probably hunting. It was a very cold winter. Snow fell constantly and the heavy cover created problems for the deer that were always hungry. Often they came right up to our mess hall, and the cooks were kind enough to feed them. Because of the wildlife in the area and the heavy snow cover, we were warned of the dangers of wandering off into the forest alone. No one ever did, including me. My sense of wanderlust was quickly stifled by the chilling temperatures, but especially by the eerie sounds that came out of the forest each night.

In spite of being exhausted most of the time, we managed to have some fun. Priest Lake was just down the hill from our work camp, and I remember taking walks by the lake with my buddies in my free time. The lake was one of the most beautiful places I had ever been. We sat by the lake smoking cigarettes, sharing stories about home, and memorizing every square inch of the beauty that surrounded us. Even at such a young age, I wisely used every single moment of my spare time to absorb and explore the world around me.

The barracks had an entertainment room with a piano and a couple of guitars. Willie and I played guitar and sang sad songs like *Old Shep*, and the rest of the guys would join in. Many nights the sounds of music and laughter filled that old hall. Willie and I were becoming good friends now. He was assigned to my crew and drove us all to and from work. He built our campfires, kept fresh coffee brewing all day long, and served lunch at camp.

There was a guy named Larry in our camp who ate bugs, and strangely we thought it was funny. I was never sure why he ate bugs, but we found it amusing and egged him on. We'd offer him cigarettes for his efforts; for example, we'd give him one cigarette for eating a moth, two cigarettes for eating a spider, and so on. The larger the insect, the greater the prize. Once, when we had spaghetti for dinner, he took a whole handful of worms and mixed them into his spaghetti. His was the only spaghetti that moved by itself. I will never forget that. We probably paid him a whole pack of Bull Durham for that one.

12

Back Home Again

When our six-month hitch with the CCC was over, we were shipped home. Willie and I traveled together in the train cross country to Reading, reminiscing about Idaho, and making plans to go fishing together when we got home. Lumberjacking had been a great adventure, and I was healthier now than I had been in a long time. By now Willie and I had become good friends, and I would spend a lot of time at his house when we got back.

Soon after we arrived in Reading, I met Willie's parents. I called them mom and pop probably because Willie did. Mom quickly grew fond of me and was good to me, but Pop only tolerated me. He was afraid I might want to date one of his daughters, and he generally disapproved of most men who showed any interest in dating his daughters.

Mom and Pop had five daughters, Betty, Evelyn, Erma, Verna and Helen, and three sons, Harold, Fred, and, of course, Willie. Helen was the only one of Willie's siblings I didn't meet because she was confined to a hospital in Philadelphia, where she had had a lung removed. She was just a toddler when doctors accidentally collapsed one of her lungs with ether during a tonsillectomy. Hospitalized, she became gravely ill as her lung began to deteriorate.

Thus began a series of operations in which doctors slowly removed her lung, lobe by lobe, until the entire organ was eventually gone. She later told me stories about how she was wheeled into a large operating arena that had rows and rows of seats located in the upper portion near the ceiling. The seats were always filled with 'spectators' as she called them. I'm sure the spectators were really doctors and other medical personnel there to observe this unique, one-of-a-kind operation.

By some miracle Helen survived many operations over a period of ten years. Much like me, she, too, grew up in a hospital, away from her family. At the age of eleven, she weighed a mere forty pounds. By the age of twelve, she was finally well enough to return home to live with her family. The very first time I met Helen, she was thirteen years old.

Not long after we came home from the CCC, Willie got himself a job at Mohn Brothers Hat factory in Reading. They were looking for more help, so Willie took me along one day and I was hired on the spot. I learned the various operations of hat making, but specialized in stiffening of hat brims by applying chemicals. I was living with Aunt Margaret at the time and took my paycheck home to her to help out, keeping a few dollars for myself.

Aunt Margaret had lost her husband by now and was struggling to make ends meet. Many people were poor in those days, struggling to survive the depression years, and Willie's family was no exception. My small paycheck was a godsend to a very grateful Aunt Margaret, who was feeding her own two boys and me as well. She'd packed a lunch for me each day to take along to the hat factory. Almost always, I'd find my favorite hard-boiled egg and mayonnaise sandwich. Nothing was ever too much trouble for Aunt Margaret when it involved her boys. I was grateful.

The hat factory was located across the alley from Willie's back yard. During lunch break Willie and I would take our lunches outside, enjoying a little fresh air and comradery while we ate. Often, Helen came outside to sit with us. She was just thirteen years old and very thin from having been ill for so many years. Willie loved his little sister and protected her with his life, and she, in turn, idolized him. Interestingly, each time Helen came out to sit with us, she planted her slender little backside right next to me, saying very little. Her gaze was palpable as she watched me with her grey-blue eyes.

I was foolishly smitten with Rosemary at the time and never expected that Helen's infatuation with me was anything other than that of a friend. She was still very much a young girl. I was fond of and cared about her simply because she was my best friend's sister. Only later would I learn that she only had eyes for me. For Helen, it was love at first sight.

Willie and I spent the next two years making hats, playing guitar and singing, fishing, and going to the movies with the girls. Rosemary and I were good friends, and we eventually became engaged. I bought her a diamond solitaire ring from Tyack's Jewelry store in Reading when I was just seventeen. However, the engagement didn't last very long. One day she got really angry, took off the ring and threw it at me. I suppose I should have attempted reconciliation, but instead I took the ring back to Tyack's and got my money back. I was never really sure why she was so angry with me, but I think it had to do with the fact that I spent more time fishin' than smoochin'. Carp fishing was a hell of a lot more fun than holding hands all the time.

By now Willie had saved enough money to buy himself a car, an old Ford with a rumble seat, so we were able to go fishing often. We fished mostly at Moselem Springs and sometimes in the Susquehanna River. Once when we were fishing at night, we cast our baited lines out into the water and settled down to wait for a bite. We were pretty comfortable lying there propped up on the seats we removed from Willie's car, with our fishing rods propped over our bellies. So comfortable, in fact, that we soon fell asleep.

We awoke at daybreak thinking it was strange we hadn't gotten a bite all night. After all, night fishing was usually the best time to catch fish. We soon realized that we had thrown our lines clear across the Maiden Creek and onto the bank on the other side.

Willie and I had a lot of fun together during the two years since we came back from the CCC. However, I had been thinking about joining the Army. I had a strong sense of adventure and felt like I was going nowhere fast working in a hat factory. I knew the military could provide me with a lot of opportunities, so I made the decision to join as soon as I turned eighteen. Willie decided he would join up too.

PART TWO

13
The Army

On August 2, 1941, I went down to the Post Office at 5th and Washington Streets with the intention of joining the military. Today was my birthday; I was 18 years old. When I walked in the front door I saw a Marine Sergeant in uniform sitting at a recruiting desk. He looked at me and asked if I would like to join up. I said that I would and went over and sat down next to him. He looked me over and said, "Do you feel alright?" I replied that I felt fine and just had a cold and runny nose. He felt my forehead and told me I had a fever. "Well," he said, "you go home and get yourself some rest, and when you feel better come back and we'll sign you up."

Needless to say, I was disappointed. My slight frame and frail appearance certainly did not appear to be what the Marines wanted. However, a poster across the room with a large hand pointing a finger in my direction indicated that someone named Uncle Sam wanted me. So I went over. Another Sergeant greeted me and said, "Hey, how are doing?" "Good," I replied, "but I've got a cold." He asked me if I was interested in joining the Army. "You wouldn't take me if I was," I replied. "The Marine over there touched my head and said I have a fever, I look flushed, and I'm sick." The Sergeant looked me up and down and said, "Don't listen to those guys, there isn't a damned thing wrong with you, son, you look okay to me." Things were looking up.

"Sit down," he said, "I'd like to ask you a few questions." I sat down across from him and looked directly into his eyes. "Were you ever in the Boy Scouts?" he inquired. "Yes," I said, "but I got kicked out because I couldn't afford the dues." "Do you like adventure?" he asked, raising one eyebrow. "Oh boy, I really like adventure," I answered, and I was about due for a new one. He asked, "Do you like to camp out?" Again I answered in the affirmative. "How about travel; do you like to go to far away places?" "The farther, the better," I said, nodding excitedly. The next thing I knew he was signing me up!

A few days passed, however, before the paperwork was finalized. During the physical exam, the doctors learned that I had had tuberculosis of the spine when I was a child, and they wanted a letter from Dr. Bisbing before they accepted me into the Army. The letter arrived quickly, and I was on my way! The Army wasted no time sending me to Fort Slocum, New York, where I was sworn in as a Private in the United States Army!

* * * * *

Soon after I enlisted in the Army, Willie went into the Army Air Force. He became a crew chief, checking out the overall mechanics of the plane and flying bombing missions with his crew over Europe in a B-17. His plane was struck by enemy fire on several occasions, but he survived the war and eventually came back home to his family. I didn't see him again until the war was over.

My brother, John, joined the Navy two years after I went into the Army. John, who was four years younger than I, was just sixteen years old when he enlisted. He wanted to get away from a difficult home life, so our father consented to his enlistment by saying he was seventeen years old.

John re-enlisted after his first hitch in WWII, serving in the U.S. Navy for a total of nine years, ultimately achieving the rank of IC1 (Interior Communications First Class). He became a Gyro Compass Specialist and a skilled electrician, serving on the following ships: NTS Sampson, USS Iowa, USS Hancock, PSC USNB, USS English, USS Sierra, and the USS Watts DD-567. He saw action in the Pacific and experienced the devastation of having his ship hit by kamikaze planes.

While serving on the USS Iowa, John met and shook the hand of President Roosevelt during Roosevelt's trip to Yalta for the conference with Churchill and Stalin. Because of Roosevelt's disability, he required a great deal of assistance getting around the ship, so the men serving on board carried the President and his wheelchair wherever he needed to go. John was proud to have had the opportunity to meet and serve the President.

In much the same way that Willie and I were proud to have served in the Army, John was always proud to have served in the Navy. John and I wouldn't see each other again until the war was over.

14
Panama Canal

On September 4, 1941, after receiving uniforms and immunizations, I was shipped from Fort Slocum in Long Island Sound to Panama. A few hundred men boarded the SS Panama, a tourist class ship that had been recently acquired by the Army and refitted to carry troops. I saw the Statue of Liberty for the first time in my life and was thrilled to be out on the ocean.

Five days at sea passed quickly, and we arrived in Panama on the 9th of September. I remember standing on the bow of the ship and pulling a photograph from my shirt pocket. After taking one long last look, I tore it into a dozen pieces and tossed it into the sea. I would never see Rosemary again.

We docked in Colon on the Caribbean side of Panama and were given a short leave to go into town. We arrived in the morning, disembarked, and were instructed to be back on board before the end of the day. Colon was unlike any place I had ever been before. Vendors sold monkeys, lizards, and parrots right on the streets. My buddies and I covered as much ground as possible, sightseeing, grabbing a bite to eat and a couple of beers. We stayed out of trouble and made sure we were back on board ship with time to spare. Proud to finally be in the Army, I had a great deal of respect for its rules. I was having the time of my life, and nothing was going to spoil it for me.

The SS Panama left Colon the following morning and sailed into the Panama Canal. An engineering masterpiece, the canal connects the Atlantic and Pacific Oceans via locks and the huge man-made Gatun Lake. We traveled through locks which raised and lowered our ship as we traversed the fifty mile long canal toward Panama City. After docking at Balboa, we were taken by truck to Fort Clayton, the base of the 33rd Infantry Regiment.

I was assigned to Company D of the 33rd Infantry and went into recruit training almost immediately. Training was tougher than I'd expected, mostly because of the heat. The humidity in Panama made August at home feel like spring. Fort Clayton was bustling with activity, and to my fascination and delight, there was a mule pack unit here in camp. There was also a Coast Guard Artillery unit and some Army engineers stationed here. Training began almost immediately and I quickly became fit for the first time in my life.

Weapons' training was the highlight of each day. In spite of the fact that I had very little formal education, I was a quick study, easily absorbing every possible aspect of handling, firing and maintaining weapons. I was like a sponge, taking in every bit of information that came my way, and there was so much to learn here in Panama. In spite of my exhaustive training regimen, my life was finally taking a turn for the better, and because I enjoyed it so much, I became proficient with many infantry weapons in no time at all. Before I knew it, I was qualified with the British Enfield Rifle; Springfield Rifle;

Bayonet; .45 caliber pistol; .30 caliber water-cooled machine gun; .30 & .50 caliber air-cooled machine guns; 60 mm mortar; 81 mm mortar; fragmentation, percussion, and smoke hand grenades.

Recruit training also included close order drill, manual of arms, techniques of marching, physical fitness and familiarization of military terms and orders. The training was thorough, intense and exhausting, and I loved it. Completion of recruit training was cause for celebration and our unit commander rewarded us with some time off. Break time, however, amounted to no more than a few days before we began the next phase of Army life—jungle warfare training.

During jungle warfare training, I was assigned to transit duty guarding vessels entering and traveling through the Panama Canal, from the Pacific to the Caribbean, and back again on another vessel the following day. Armed with a .45 caliber pistol, I kept a watchful eye for any movement along the locks or on the water in a 90 degree radius. Additional men covered the remaining areas of the ship. I also carried what we called a sawed-off shotgun. The weapon, which had a shortened barrel and delivered a powerful blast of shot, was an excellent deterrent to any unauthorized individuals who came too close to the locks.

Our detachment was taken out to sea on a military speedboat to meet the ship we were assigned to guard. Crew members would drop a ladder down the bow of the ship for us to board. Assigned to strategic locations on the ship, we saw it safely through the entire Canal. We were most diligent when going through the locks where opportunities for sabotage were greatest. Sailing on open water was much less risky; here is where we had an opportunity to eat, relax or have a smoke. Our orders were to shoot anyone who threw anything into the locks.

At the end of our journey, we disembarked and spent the night at Fort Davis. The next morning, we'd begin the process all over again, boarding and guarding another ship going to the Pacific. The months I served on canal duty were without incident and I never had to pull the trigger in defense of a ship, though I know that I'd have done my duty. Some of the men found canal duty dull and routine, but I found it stimulating and interesting and was proud that I was given the responsibility of protecting the ships. I was only 18 years old, and for the first time in my life, I felt really important.

We were constantly in training, alternating jungle training with transit duty on the Canal, a week or two in the jungles, a week on the Canal, then back to the jungle again. We were becoming fine-tuned soldiers.

Each squad of seven men was assigned a mule to carry our weapons, ammunition and necessary supplies into and out of the jungle during warfare training. My squad was given a large black mule named Devil. I was very excited to have an animal to care for and wanted the job of mule leader. Being fond of horses, I figured a mule wouldn't be much different; however, within a very short period of time, Devil taught me the many differences between horses and mules, and most importantly, who was really in charge of whom.

Keep in mind, I was a horse lover, but there were days when I wanted to kill that mule. He was a large Missouri mule with an even bigger attitude. I'd never known a man or beast to be more ornery, and to make matters worse, Army rules forbade striking or abusing our mules in any fashion whatsoever. The consequences were dire, and that damned mule knew it.

As mule leader, I was responsible for leading the mule to and from training, but every man in the squad was responsible for feeding and caring for Devil. Mules, which are not usually found in tropical climates, are more comfortable in much cooler temperatures, which likely explains his ill temperament. After a day in the jungle with us, he'd be hot, sweaty, and filthy. Our job back at camp was to cool him off, rub him down, then water and feed him. He always came first. Only after Devil was taken care of were we allowed to get ourselves cleaned up and fed.

Needless to say, Devil was well cared for, and he showed his appreciation by being as disagreeable as possible, balking, biting, kicking, and just plain refusing to work. Just getting him harnessed, loaded, and moving in a forward direction was exhausting.

It may seem crazy, but I wanted to spend more time around the mules, so I volunteered to help clean up the stables on weekends. Any man who volunteered for barn duty was rewarded by being allowed to ride his squad's mule in his free time. I made several foolish attempts to ride Devil, but each time I entered his stall, he pinned me against the wall and wouldn't budge. In a desperate attempt to avoid being crushed on a few occasions, I punched him a couple of times, though fortunately I was never caught. Devil was the first and only mule that I ever attempted to ride.

Our jungle warfare training continued, and it was tough; everything worked against us. The dense vegetation was full of snakes, lizards and all kinds of insects flying and jumping all over the place. The mosquitoes were especially bad, and the heat and humidity were oppressive. We were training and trying to survive at the same time.

Surviving jungle warfare meant mastering one crucial skill, the element of surprise. We'd break up into small groups and take advantage of the natural camouflage to avoid each other. Sneaking up and ambushing our own men made the training seem more like a game than the serious business that it would become in the months ahead. Learning to remain undetected while ambushing the 'enemy' would hopefully save our lives some day. At the end of each day's activities, we returned to camp worn out, but wiser than the day before.

In spite of the fact that I have an excellent memory, I lack the ability to remember names. However, there are two that I have not forgotten: Lieutenant Coffee, and Sergeant Bean. There you have it, Coffee—Bean. The only explanation I have for remembering the names of these two men, both of whom I admired, is that coffee has always been the mainstay of my life. There were times when it kept me warm and times when it kept me alive. I am certain that coffee flows through the veins in my body.

Lieutenant Coffee, a West Pointer, was our Company Commander. Every one of us had a great deal of respect for him because he was a fair man and a good officer who treated us well, built our confidence, always looked out for us, and taught us to be proud of ourselves. Under his command we were becoming better men and competent soldiers, as well.

Sergeant Bean was our mess sergeant. He was a funny guy who frequently entertained us during meals with his own style of stand-up comedy. He polled us for our favorite food items when ordering supplies for the mess kitchen, and periodically surprised us at dinner with an oversized birthday cake in celebration of any of us who had an upcoming birthday. Dinner in the mess hall was transformed into a special event as every man joined in a rousing chorus of *Happy Birthday to You.* Sergeant Bean operated a first-class mess hall and was well liked by every man who ever had the good fortune to know him.

All the men here in Fort Clayton were regular Army, men who had volunteered to be here, and our officers were all West Pointers. Because we had a lot in common, the men got along quite well, and the days passed quickly. After three months of training, Company D was ordered to pack up and ship out. I was somewhat sorry to leave Panama; my time here had been a great adventure.

We would not be informed of our destination until we were on board ship and well underway. Early on the morning of December 6, 1941, we boarded an old WWI troop ship, sailed through the Panama Canal one last time, and headed for the Caribbean. When we reached open sea, we were finally given our orders. We were headed to Trinidad in the British

West Indies to build a base and establish a military presence on the island.

The Army was becoming a family to me, or at least what I perceived a family to be, a home base, literally. The Army cared about me, fed me and gave me a home and a feeling of security. I finally belonged to something now, something good. I found my new life exciting and eagerly looked forward to whatever lay ahead.

15
Trinidad, British West Indies

One day out of Panama, we were given the news that the Japanese had bombed Pearl Harbor. The day was December 7, 1941. I was sitting on the bow of the ship cleaning my rifle when I heard the announcement over the ship's loudspeaker. I was very young and hadn't really thought much about the events that were occurring around the world.

I wasn't aware that eighteen months ago President Franklin D. Roosevelt had sent a fleet of battleships to Pearl Harbor in an attempt to deter the Japanese from making aggressive moves into the East Indies and Southeast Asia. The Japanese needed oil and raw materials to support an ongoing war they started with China in 1937. Western powers had halted trade with Japan in July of 1941, and Japan was becoming desperate enough to take what it needed.

However, in a well-executed assault, the Japanese turned the tables by eliminating the threat, the entire U.S. fleet, from Pearl Harbor in a massive sneak attack that occurred before 8:00 AM on this fateful day. I would soon learn that five of our eight battleships had been sunk, and the remaining three were badly damaged. Other ships were damaged, as well, and many planes on the ground were destroyed. Twenty-four hundred Americans were dead. I felt frightened by this news and deeply saddened for the loss of so many lives. I stopped cleaning my rifle and stared intensely at the gloomy horizon that was beginning to look as ominous as the thought that just entered my mind; war was now inevitable.

A few hours later, we encountered an awful storm. High winds hit us from the north. We were only on the fringe of the storm, but it was rough nonetheless. The waves rose higher and higher until the bow went completely underwater. The storm, which lasted most of the night, took its toll on the men. Our thoughts went from the tragedy at Pearl Harbor to hanging on for our own dear lives. I didn't get sick; I don't know why.

We arrived in Port of Spain, Trinidad a day or so later, accompanied by clear skies and calm seas. The site chosen for our base in Trinidad was one of six sites that President Roosevelt obtained from Britain in September of 1940 in his 'freighters for bases' deal. Roosevelt negotiated free 99-year leases in exchange for fifty old U.S. destroyers. The destroyers would help Britain in its war against Germany, and the bases near South America would enable the United States to protect the Panama Canal while monitoring and deterring German U-boat activity along the South American coastline.

German U-boats were targeting British supply ships transporting goods from South America. Rubber was just one of many crucial products being shipped to England. Roosevelt felt that war with Germany was inevitable and wanted to be prepared. He was right; on the 11th of December we were given the news that Germany declared war against the United States.

The next several months kept us busy building a base camp near Port of Spain. We called it Dockside Camp. The construction of this base was urgent business that kept us busy with little time for anything else. Presently there was just one company of us, plus Officers, mess, supply, and medical personnel. We were the first American military personnel stationed on the island. We set up camp by the water near Port of Spain and slept in tents; eight men per tent. Fortunately, our arrival in Trinidad coincided with the end of the rainy season, so the weather was mostly dry while we built our Camp. Our primary duty at this time was to guard and protect our equipment and supplies.

Supplies were constantly being brought to the island and additional military personnel arrived daily, as well. Medical units arrived and set up a field hospital. Army Engineers began building a runway and warehouses for storage. Several months passed before the camp was up and running, but eventually it shaped up very nicely.

We began training again, alternating training with guarding stockpiles of equipment and supplies that grew larger by the day. Materials like diesel oil, gasoline and motor oil were crucial to the operation of the base and were guarded round the clock. Building a military base from the ground up was a massive undertaking, and I was proud to be part of it.

Eventually, in conjunction with our guard duty, we moved into the jungles to continue our jungle warfare training. We set up an outpost that served as our base while in training. This involved clearing some very dense vegetation. The clearing was done by hand with our bolo knives and had to be repeated almost daily. Our outpost was primitive but comfortable; we slept in hammocks strung from trees with mosquito netting for cover. Cooking consisted mostly of C-type rations that were prepared over campfires. We honed our survival skills daily. Training in the jungle was the ultimate adventure, and living there was almost serene. I longed for one thing only—Aunt Laura's home cooking.

Operating from our outpost, we were sent into the jungle in small groups of eight or nine men for days at a time. Most of our training was conducted in the rainforests of northern Trinidad, but eventually we spread out over much of the island. We encountered many native people during our training. Some were friendly toward us, others indifferent, but none were ever hostile, and I found the culture to be a fascinating study. Many of the natives had never ventured out of their own villages, yet seemed very content with their simple lives. I often saw merchants going into the hills with mules loaded with staples like sugar and rice to trade with the villagers for cocoa beans, much like hucksters back home bringing fresh produce up and down city streets. Trinidad was completely captivating, and I was thrilled to be here.

On our treks into the jungle, we took with us only D-bars, matches, and basic weapons, one canteen of water, a few survival items, and the clothes we were wearing. We were given no food to take with us. Fresh water, sometimes difficult to find, always had to be treated with iodine; however, fruits were easy enough to locate as they grew abundantly throughout the jungle. Coconut milk was a favorite of mine, and I relished the nut as well. Finding meat was an entirely different matter.

As part of our training, we were taught to identify the island's edible flora and fauna. Our greatest challenge lay in finding these edibles, and in the case of fauna, catching and preparing it. We also learned to identify edible insects and grubs, and how to distinguish and avoid poisonous indigenous reptiles and insects. A few men in my Company suffered snake bites and became ill, but none of them died from it. As for me, I couldn't resist the temptation to handle such beautiful creatures, the Bushmaster included. I only handled youngsters, and usually by the tail. Fortunately, I was never bitten.

We ate anything we could get our hands on. Iguana, a large tropical lizard commonly found on the island, was a favorite among the locals, so we figured it must be tasty. We figured wrong. We caught our first Iguana by outrunning it. After cutting off its head and removing the entrails, we skinned it, built a spit, and roasted the carcass over a fire. Because we wanted to be sure the strange flesh was completely cooked, we overcooked the meat. It became dried out and blackened beyond recognition, but we ate it nevertheless. I was real hungry that night, but I didn't go for seconds.

We occasionally ate grubs, filled with liquid, sort of like little éclairs. I didn't make a habit of it, only when I was very hungry. Mostly we picked breadfruit, wild bananas, limes, mangoes, and papayas. Fresh fruit was delicious and grew everywhere. We caught fish with hand lines and roasted the fresh meat over an open fire. It was always delicious. Occasionally the guys shot a monkey for the meat; I didn't. I didn't shoot them and I didn't eat them. That's where I drew the line.

We bought a small pig from a native village. The villagers balked at first, not wanting to part with the animal, but we had visions of barbequed spare ribs in our brains and were desperate for some meat after days of eating fruit and grubs. When we resorted to groveling, the natives finally agreed to share the meat with us under the condition that they keep the best parts. "Okay, alright!" responded an eager chorus of hungry men; some pig was better than none.

We stood nearby and watched as one villager held the pig and a second disemboweled it. Had I not been so ravenous, I might have felt sorry for the critter. The natives quickly butchered the little fellow, keeping the head, feet and entrails for themselves. Then to our complete astonishment, they handed the carcass to us. Only slightly disappointed that we wouldn't be having pig's feet jelly on our morning toast, we ecstatically accepted the skinny, but wonderful carcass that was dressed and ready to cook, then skewered and roasted it to perfection.

The delectable aroma of freshly roasted pig hung low in the humid night air, evoking memories of Aunt Laura's kitchen. I closed my eyes and thought back to those days as I feasted on the succulent meat. We pulled off the outsides; it was tender and crisp. The meat on the inside was still a little raw, but it didn't matter. There was plenty of cooked meat for all of us. That was a feast I will never forget.

Back at Dockside Camp on a brief break from jungle training, Lieutenant Coffee summoned me to his office one day and asked me if I could "whip the ass of any man" in my squad. "No, Sir, I can't," I blurted out to him without thinking about my answer first. "Too bad," he said, "then you're not ready to be squad leader." "Damn," I murmured a bit too loudly. I could easily have handled the job of squad leader, and whipped a few asses too, I thought to myself. Disappointed, I decided the next time I would choose my words more carefully. Eventually I ascended to that role and others, but not on that day.

On a beach just outside of Dockside Camp lay a rusted old freighter that had run aground many years prior. When the tide went out, my buddy, Private First Class Joseph Miller, and I would climb up on the deck and fish with heavy hand lines, using raw meat for bait. Fishing was a respite from training, freeing my mind of what was to come. The waters below us teemed with tropical fish in colors I never knew existed. Watching them glide and dart, shimmering in the tropical sunlight, was mesmerizing and distracting, so much so that one day I was nearly dragged overboard by an enormous ray that had taken my bait. The manta had a wingspan that was greater than my height and in spite of the fact that I could never have landed such a fine specimen under my present circumstances, I refused to let go of the line. In lieu of jumping into the water to save my life, Joe made a snap decision to cut the line and, to my great disappointment, we watched the magnificent creature glide away in the crystal clear water. Our efforts were not in vain, however. We caught other colorful species that day, most of which we could not identify, then returned them safely to the water.

A Marine unit was stationed on the island by now, so we took advantage of the opportunity to work with them. Small boats ferried a few dozen men at a time out to a couple of large merchant ships about a mile off shore. We practiced loading and unloading for assault landings. During these exercises we carried our full gear and weapons. Moving quickly, we climbed several stories straight up a rope ladder and onto the deck of the ship. Still moving quickly, we made our way across deck and down a rope ladder on the other side of the ship into a waiting boat that whisked us right back to where we started. Boys being boys, we taunted the Marines and they dished it right back to us. "You're nothing but a bunch of pussies," they'd tell us. Because we were supervised the entire time, the exchange resulted in nothing more than banter. We climbed up and down those ladders in the hot sun for the better part of the day, carrying our heavy gear, until we were exhausted. That completed, we practiced landing approaches on a small island in the area.

Whenever I could get my hands on a pass, I'd go into Port of Spain to a bar for a few drinks and a few laughs with my buddies Ted and Joe. We three were instigators when we had a few drinks in us, and we occasionally got ourselves into trouble, especially when British sailors were in town. In spite of the fact that our nations were allies, the trouble inevitably began as banter after we had a bit too much to drink, and escalated into a full scale row, with flying fists, tables and chairs. The instigators generally started with name calling, specifically about Yanks or Uncle Sam, and then we would counter with a few choice comments of our own about their Queen. "You bloody Yanks are overfed, overpaid and oversexed," I remember one drunken sailor shouting in my direction. "Ah, go fuck yourself and your Queen while you're at it, you goddamned limeys," I'd tell them as my buddies teetered precariously on their stools, laughing hysterically. That would really piss off the Brits and all hell would break loose. The MP's would break us up and drag us all back to camp, and short of a minor scolding from Lieutenant Coffee, I don't ever recall being disciplined.

Private First Class Ted Jemison acquired a small monkey that he kept as a pet. He bought it from a street-corner vendor in Port of Spain for a few dollars. The transaction was an impulse one evening after we'd had too much to drink, but seemed like a good idea at the time. Ted frequently indulged the monkey by giving him Cheese-it crackers and beer, two of the monkey's favorite treats. We'd take him along with us to the club in Port of Spain, set him on the bar, and buy him a beer. He'd sit there quietly drinking and no one seemed to mind that there was a monkey on the bar. A few times he had a bit too much to drink and got a little rowdy, so we took him back to camp. He'd stagger around like a drunken soldier for a little while, then lie down and go to sleep. One night he got really drunk and the next morning Ted found him stiff as a board. We really felt bad about that.

The population at Dockside Camp was growing and occasional problems occurred with personnel. The Army was generally intolerant of disobedience, and generous in meting out punishment. I witnessed this when I was assigned to guard a prisoner from another unit. We were occasionally assigned as prison chasers, which meant guarding prisoners on work details. Prisoners with minor crimes were assigned five or six to a guard. Those who had committed more serious crimes were assigned an individual guard.

I was assigned one prisoner, a soldier from a trucking company who raped a native girl. He was found guilty, court martialed, and given a prison sentence of ninety-nine years.

He was awaiting shipment to Fort Leavenworth, Kansas, when he was turned over to me. I was instructed to hold no conversations with him, to give him water from time to time, and to 'run him' from job to job. No breaks, no privileges. If he tried to run, I had orders to shoot him, and I would not have hesitated; I had no sympathy for the man. He was not shackled or handcuffed, but fortunately I was armed with a .45. He asked me one day what I would do if he ran. I looked him squarely in the eyes and told him to "try it." He never attempted to escape and, much to my relief, he was shipped out the following week.

Malaria was common in Trinidad, not so much with military personnel, but widespread with the locals. We were given a quinine tablet every day to protect us, but I got careless and didn't take it as often as I should have, especially when I was on training missions. Quinine dulled my senses, caused a ringing in my ears, and affected my hearing as well. Needless to say, I was one of only a few guys who got malaria. I became ill very suddenly and remained very sick for days with high fevers, chills, and trembling. Sent to Dockside Camp aid station for treatment, I was given quinine, lots of water, and a bunk in a lonely corner where I suffered it out for a few weeks. After I recovered, I was much more careful about taking the quinine, having learned a difficult lesson. Even though relapses were common, I only ever had one recurrence of the disease.

Eventually the Army switched us from quinine tablets to Atabrine. I remember taking the bright yellow bitter tasting tablets that were thought to stave off malaria. Atabrine was, in fact, later proven to be effective, but the men didn't like taking it; we felt like guinea pigs. It caused some of the guys to vomit, and turned others a sickly shade of yellow. No one wanted to take it, including me. Most of the men were willing to risk malaria than have their skin turn yellow. However, once the dosage was adjusted, the symptoms almost completely disappeared. I would soon be shipped back to the States and off to Europe and fortunately wouldn't have to take it for very much longer.

While on patrol one morning, training on a beach, I stepped on a piece of bamboo. It pierced my right foot deeply between my first and second toes, and within a couple of days became infected. The foot was grossly swollen and rigid and I couldn't walk on it anymore, creating a serious problem for my squad. I needed treatment but couldn't walk. Because the terrain was so mountainous and we were miles from camp, it was impossible for the men to carry me back, so they took me to a fishing village nearby, where several villagers agreed to take me back to camp by boat.

Two of the men in my squad lifted me carefully into the vessel, an ancient dugout type of boat complete with oars. It was hand made, crude but swift, and sliced easily through the water, delivering me to the other side of the island where the Army could pick me up and take me for treatment. Because we were a great distance from camp, the trip by boat took several hours. Too distressed to enjoy the scenery, I was relieved when we finally reached the point of pick up because I was beginning to feel ill.

The infection was a bad one, persistent even though the wound was treated with sulfa. I was given the standard APC pills for pain, but they were completely worthless. Only after someone got the bright idea to place my leg in an elevated position did the swelling begin to go down. Again, I was laid up for a couple of weeks, but soon recovered completely.

In spite of the illnesses, injuries, rashes, fungal infections and other discomforts I experienced in Trinidad, I absolutely loved the jungle and spent my free time taking in the scenery, especially the sounds of birds and insects and the smell of humid vegetation. There were hundreds of species of brilliant birds, insects, moths and butterflies, and orchids in every color grew among the trees and vines. Ferns in the most vivid shades of green grew in abundance throughout the rainforest, sated by gentle afternoon rains that fell daily throughout the rainy season. The jungle was truly a paradise.

Vampire bats, which feed on the blood of mammals, flew freely each night in search of a meal, posing no threat to us. I had always imagined them to be enormous creatures stalking humans soon after the sun set; to my surprise, they were tiny little mammals that had no interest in humans whatsoever. Particularly intrigued with scorpions also, I enjoyed the occasional challenge of sparring with one until it lashed out at me with the stinger at the end of its tail, striking whatever object I had in my hand.

My squad encountered a lot of snakes. Because many of the species in Trinidad are arboreal, snakes could easily be found resting or hunting in trees. I enjoyed hunting for snakes. I'd pick them up carefully by the tail and play with them, but most of the guys wanted nothing to do with snakes. I thought they were beautiful creatures; the guys thought I was nuts. When Army engineers cleared vegetation for our runway, they inadvertently killed a 28-foot Anaconda when they ran over it with a bulldozer. The carcass, a foot in diameter, was given to some locals who skinned it and preserved the hide.

I found a young anaconda and kept it as a pet. It was about three feet long and I carried it around with me for a few months, mostly wearing it around my neck. My little anaconda was colorful, docile and never bit me. During the day it scouted around camp, probably foraging for a mouse or lizard for lunch, but it never left the area. It curled up in my bunk with me at night, and during training I'd put it in my hammock and zip the mosquito netting closed until I returned to camp. After a few months, however, I released the snake back to the jungle.

I had a great deal of respect for jungle creatures. Even though I handled many of them, I was always careful not to harm them. One exception was tarantulas. I saw one now and then, but the only time I ever handled one was to remove it from my chest, and I did that with little regard for its safety. I was resting against a palm tree on a beach during a break from training one morning, eyes closed, completely relaxed, when it found its way up my torso. The sensation of a feathery object lightly stroking my chest woke me abruptly. And just in time. The tarantula which sat calmly on my upper chest was reaching for my chin, sending me into a spin. Lightning doesn't move as fast as I did the morning I flung that tarantula off my chest. I regret now that I killed the spider, but it seemed the right thing to do at the time.

Stationed in Trinidad from December of 1941 until the middle of August 1943 in continuous training, we were finally told to pack; we were shipping out. I would miss the country that taught me so much, but felt excited about what lay ahead. We had built our base from the ground up, establishing America's military presence in the region. But the time had arrived for my Company to move on. We were headed back to the States, but I would always remember this country where I experienced so much.

16
The Fighting 69th
Camp Shelby, Mississippi

We left Trinidad for the United States with a stopover in Puerto Rico. Our ship docked in San Juan and we were driven by truck to Fort Buchanan for a ten-day layover. Because of our extensive jungle training in Panama and Trinidad, the Army asked for volunteers to go to China and Burma. Some of the men volunteered; I didn't. This was the only time in my Army career that I did not volunteer. Those who did were shipped out immediately and ultimately became part of the famous unit known as Merrill's Marauders.

While on leave in San Juan, our company commander gave us some time to tour the island. Anyone interested in seeing the sights was loaded into trucks and driven around the island where we visited a large prison and the University of Puerto Rico. I was more interested in the scenery and vegetation. Though not as dense or lush as Trinidad, the vegetation in Puerto Rico was beautiful, and there was an ever-present breeze coming in from the ocean.

Our tour lasted only a few hours, and then we were dropped off and given free time to roam around San Juan. Of course, we were warned to stay out of trouble, and as a precaution, we were instructed by our Company Commander to carry our trench knives with us at all times. Not really expecting any trouble, we did as we were told and tucked them into our boots. Most of my time in San Juan was spent walking the streets with a couple of my buddies, having a look around, drinking good rum, and checking out the locals. Our time there was relaxing and passed quickly, and before we realized ten days had passed, we were told to pack and ready ourselves to go home.

Early morning on the day of our departure, about forty men were sitting on the bow of the ship, in uniform, participating in a Sunday morning service conducted by our Chaplain. I was sitting on the port side of the ship enjoying the service when I glanced briefly over my left shoulder for one last look at the beautiful San Juan coastline. The vista was interrupted only by a single brilliant bird gliding directly towards me. It seemed to come out of nowhere and chose to alight gracefully and purposefully onto my shoulder. My response was immediate. I chose not to move, but sat silently and gazed at the gift that I had just received. I was too mesmerized for the next minute or so to notice the awe-struck faces of my fellow shipmates. The small parrot-like bird was multi-colored and never made a sound. After resting quietly on my shoulder for about a minute, it lifted off in the direction of the island and disappeared almost as quickly and magically as it had appeared. Not one word was spoken by anyone, including our Chaplain, during this brief but wonderful interlude.

The remainder of our journey home was agreeable in both weather and company. Upon our return to the States, we docked at New Orleans, disembarked, and were given free time to go into town. My buddies and I walked the narrow streets of the French Quarter with its colorful houses, shuttered windows, and French doors. Narrow alleys led to beautiful hidden gardens. I don't think we missed a single bar or strip club, and later we raised a little hell on Canal Street. It was good to be back in the States.

It was now September of 1943. From our distribution compound in New Orleans we were loaded into trucks and taken to Fort McClellan, Alabama for a brief stay. Then we were split up and sent to different forts and camps. I was sent to Camp Shelby, Mississippi, home of the Fighting 69th Infantry Division known as Bolty's Bivouacking Bastards, where I was put into Company D, 272nd Regiment. I remained here for about eight months.

We were constantly training: forced marches, field maneuvers and playing war. One aspect of our training involved participating in maneuvers against Japanese-American units stationed there. These units were worthwhile adversaries, agile and clever, and gave us a run for our money. During maneuvers aircraft flew over our positions and dropped bombs (sacks of flour) that hit the ground and burst. Anyone in the area or covered in flour was 'dead,' then the maneuvers were judged to decide the winners from the losers. Playing soldier, especially during night maneuvers, sharpened our senses and kept us on our toes.

One forced march took us all day and part of the night into Biloxi, Mississippi a distance of more than forty miles. The cooler September air made the hike more bearable, especially since we were carrying full combat gear. We were permitted only a few short breaks and no water during the march, so we put pebbles in our mouths to increase salivation. A few guys didn't make it and dropped from exhaustion before we reached Biloxi. I was fit from all my training in Trinidad and didn't have any problem finishing the march, but I was beat when we set up camp that evening. After a restful night's sleep we were shipped back to Camp Shelby by truck the next morning.

Here is where I met George Vath, from Trevose, Pennsylvania. He was an infantry soldier, a couple of years younger than I, and we quickly became very good friends. George liked to jitterbug and I liked horses, so we spent our free time dancing with the local girls, and riding horseback around the Mississippi countryside. Consequently, I learned to jitterbug, and George learned to ride. We went into New Orleans and got matching tattoos of a shield with USA in the middle. I wrote to his family, and his mother sent us both letters and packages of homemade cookies. George and I agreed to stay in touch and looked forward to seeing each other again after the war. Finally, we said our goodbyes and parted with orders to report to a deportation area for shipment to Europe. But first we were each given an eleven-day leave to go home before shipping out.

* * * * *

While I was home on leave, I stopped by the Post Office, in uniform, and found the same Sergeant who recruited me on duty at the recruiting desk. We greeted each other cordially, and to my disappointment he did not recognize me. I said, "Do you remember me?" He shook his head and said, "No, I'm afraid I don't. A lot of people come through here." Even though I was a totally different person now, both mentally and physically, there must have been at least something about me that he might remember. Feeling a twinge of disappointment that the Sergeant didn't recognize me, I persisted. "I'm the guy who came in here two years ago who liked to go to far away places and camp out. Do you remember that?" I asked hopefully. Well, he started laughing out loud and said, "My God," and put his arm around me and shook my hand. "I want to thank you," I told him, "because you certainly got me going in the right direction." He smiled. "It was tough as a son of a bitch down there," I told him, "but it certainly made a different person out of me, and I will always be grateful to you for that."

17
England

It was spring of 1944 when I boarded a train for my brief visit at home. I hadn't seen my sister in over two years. The last two and a half years had been tough, but had given me a powerful sense of worth and a stability that I had never known before; I was proud of what I'd become.

My sister Betty was thrilled to see me and wrapped me in her arms. Her husband, Jack, was in Europe now with 1st Army Communications, so I stayed with her and her young son, John, in their small apartment on Robeson Street. Eleven days leave gave me ample time to make my rounds, with one exception, my father.

The very last time I saw my father was during that leave, but not by choice. I went into a hotel at 7th and Franklin Streets for a couple of beers and spotted my father at the other end of the bar. He was sitting by himself with a drink in his hand. I met his gaze, and then quickly looked away, but not before he said to me, "Hey soldier, what's your name?" Without looking in his direction, I sipped my beer and gave him a name, but not my real name. He continued, "I have a son somewhere down around South America, and you look just like him." I looked directly at him and replied, "Old man, you are mistaken; I am not your son." His reply was solemn as he looked at me and said, "If you are not my son, get the hell out of here." I turned on my heel and walked out.

The memories were too few and the anger too recent. I made one of the biggest mistakes of my life that afternoon as I turned my back on my father and walked out. I didn't know it then, but I would never see him again.

Upon departing Camp Shelby, I was handed shipping orders to report to Fort Dix, New Jersey, for shipment to Europe. I was destined to become an infantry replacement. My visit with Martha, Aunt Margaret, Aunt Laura and my sister, Betty, revitalized me, and I felt accomplished and prepared for what lay ahead, even though it was beyond my comprehension. I felt complete and was deeply happy for the first time in my life.

I boarded a train and left Reading, as ordered, on the twelfth day of my leave and traveled to Philadelphia, then on to Fort Dix, New Jersey. As expected, I was put into a rifle package, which meant I was officially an infantry soldier headed for the front. I would literally be replacing a soldier, perhaps younger than I, who had been injured, or worse, had made the ultimate sacrifice for his country. I was alone now; the Army had separated me from the friends I had made in Panama and Trinidad. I would soon learn that the business of war was not conducive to long term friendships; friends were lost by separation and sometimes by death.

The Army was expeditious in processing me through the necessary channels for shipment to Europe. The war was in full swing and replacements were desperately needed. In spite of the fact that I was being sent to the front, I eagerly anticipated performing the duty for which I had been trained. I was ready and needed to move on.

There were several hundred of us headed to war. Because the British were helping to transport American troops and supplies to England, we boarded a British ship, the Athlone Castle of the British Castle Lines, in New York Harbor. I was fascinated by every aspect of my journey through life, including something as insignificant as traveling by ship. The crew, the men, the ship, and the vistas offered new opportunities to absorb the world around me. It was an ongoing process.

With the exception of an excess of mutton, tea and biscuits, the Athlone Castle did not disappoint me. She was 725 ft. long and built to transport mail and passengers to Cape Town, South Africa. She sailed for the first time in 1936, and later served as a troop transport ship during WWII. I learned many years later that when the war ended the Athlone returned to her mail and passenger service to South Africa, and stayed in service until sometime in the late 1960s when she was finally retired.

We sailed past the Statue of Liberty and joined a large convoy of ships carrying troops and supplies to Europe. Our escorts were PTs (Patrol Torpedo Boats) and destroyers. PTs were the ultimate bodyguards. They were 80 feet long, could accelerate to 48 knots in eleven or twelve seconds, and packed more firepower per pound than any other ship the Navy could offer. Limited by their smaller size and fuel capacity, they were only able to escort us for a short distance into the Atlantic. The destroyers, however, stayed with us all the way to England, along with other naval ships that were assigned to protect our convoy.

It took about eleven days to cross the Atlantic. To remain safely undetected, we traveled in total blackout during the night. We spread ourselves out over a wide area and sailed erratically across the Atlantic, weaving north, then south in a zigzag fashion in order to avoid being detected by deadly German U-boats.

German U-Boats were referred to as wolf packs because, like wolves, they hunted in packs. They'd line up, patiently waiting for a convoy of ships. When a convoy was spotted, the lead submarine would follow it, reporting back pertinent details such as speed and direction to the pack. The remainder of the pack would then encircle the convoy and go in for the kill.

Occasionally a ship in our convoy would drop depth charges. The resonating sound was cause for concern, and we knew there were U-boats in the area. Mostly we just sat around hoping we wouldn't get hit by a torpedo. A few ships in our convoy fell victim to U-boats. On the horizon we watched with consternation the billowing smoke and fire of ships torpedoed and sunk along the way. We lost men just going to war.

During the war, many ships were lost to U-boats, but at great expense to the Germans who lost about eighty percent of their fleet, thanks to clever tactics of allied forces in aircraft and warships. U-boats were also lost to mines, some were missing in action, and others were scuttled by their own crew to avoid capture. After the war, however, captured U-boats were scuttled by allied forces.

Upon reaching our destination, the convoy split up dispersing ships into their assigned ports. The Athlone docked in Liverpool, and I was greatly relieved to finally be in England. We disembarked under cover of darkness and were greeted by the Salvation Army, who gave us coffee and doughnuts. What a treat to have a cup of coffee after drinking tea for the last eleven days. We soon found out that it was next to impossible to get a good cup of coffee in England.

Not long after arriving in Liverpool, I volunteered for the 101st Airborne and was sent immediately by train to Reading to begin my paratrooper training. The train made a stop in London, allowing me a brief glimpse of the city and a few hours to stretch my legs. While walking the streets of London, I reflected on the last couple of years. Opportunities in the Army seemed endless, and now I was becoming a paratrooper. In two short years I'd been to more places than most people ever dream about. And this was only the beginning!

My paratrooper training began immediately and initially involved practicing jumps from inside the fuselage of a plane sitting on the ground. Men were desperately needed for the war effort, so we were taken out for our first jump after only one week of instruction. And that was just fine with me.

Lined up inside the plane, we were told when to jump, one man at a time in quick succession. We were connected to a static line which pulled our chutes open for us after we made our jump and cleared the airplane. I was amazed by the sensation; I didn't feel like I was falling, but more like flying. We were able to speak and hear each other clearly as we were falling. My first jump was exhilarating, and the landing went smoothly. However, the ground came up to meet me a bit sooner than I'd expected and knocked me off my feet.

After picking up our chutes, we were loaded back into the planes and took off for our second jump of the day. Some of the drops were miscalculated due to a sudden wind change. About fifteen to twenty planes were involved in the drop, and the first groups to jump landed safely in a designated clearing. However, the remaining groups were not so lucky. I was part of that group.

Our parachutes, basically large round mushroom-shaped canopies, offered us very little maneuverability, especially when dropped from lower altitudes like today's jump. Even though I lacked experience as a paratrooper, I had very strong survival skills and could usually work myself out of a bad situation. But avoiding the catastrophe that was about to occur was completely out of my control.

Most of us were injured during the jump; some very seriously. Many of the men landed in trees in a heavily wooded area, and others hit farm equipment and small structures on the ground. I crashed painfully into a large tree to the sound of snapping limbs, praying they weren't my own. My 28-foot chute, which lay blossomed over the top of a very large tree, left me hanging in a mass of tangled lines and tree limbs and held me captive for what seemed like an eternity as I slowly struggled to extricate myself from a difficult situation.

Gradually managing to free myself from the chute, I fell about fifteen feet to the ground, snapping branches slowing my descent. After sucking the wind back into my lungs, I lay there for what seemed like hours, in a great deal of pain, before help arrived. The whole scene was quite a mess; many of the men had broken bones. I didn't, even though I was badly bruised and walking was painful for quite some time.

We were taken to a hospital at Warminster Barracks for treatment. I was bedridden there for a week or so, but many others were there a lot longer. While we recovered, the war went on without us, and to my great disappointment, so did the 101st Airborne.

18
Normandy, France

S till limping, but adequately recovered, I was sent by rail to Southampton for shipment to Normandy, France. A few hundred guys boarded an old converted freighter, and I didn't know any of them. While crossing the English Channel, I heard artillery fire in the distance. This was not my first exposure to the sounds of war; I knew the sound of a depth charge. That evening I watched flashes of light on the horizon over France and remember thinking it wasn't much different than a big Fourth of July celebration, only this wasn't the Fourth of July. Not too many miles ahead of us, the war was underway. Perhaps it was an excess of tea or the churning water beneath the bow, but I had an uneasy feeling in the pit of my stomach.

About a mile from Omaha Beach, we grabbed our heavy gear, climbed over the rail down rope ladders midship, and jumped onto British assault crafts. The descent was difficult due to the churning sea, requiring a great deal of concentration and balance. I'd ventured down the side of a ship before, but this time was different. The English Channel, sister to the rugged North Atlantic and equally as temperamental, was a challenging host. My kind of challenge. The landing craft ferried my group into shallow water, about three feet deep, then lowered its ramp. Moving quickly, we jumped into the water and waded ashore.

It was almost three weeks after the Normandy invasion. Wet and loaded down with gear, we were ordered to move quickly across the vast stretch of beach, maneuvering over and around what remained of the devastation of D-Day. As we worked our way about a hundred feet up a steep hill, the cold seawater sloshing around inside my boots stung my feet, still raw from the jungle rot I picked up in the British West Indies.

I turned around and looked back from the crest of the hill, over the massive beach and across the beautiful English Channel. The enormous beach was littered with debris and cluttered with equipment and vehicles. I saw no trace of the two thousand brave men who died here, but strangely, I felt their presence. An urgent and massive effort was underway to clear large areas for incoming equipment, vehicles and supplies. I was awed by the magnitude of the undertaking, yet felt a strange sadness over the loss of men I had never known.

Scanning the vista, I could visualize the carnage. There remained vehicles without drivers, weapons without holsters, boots and helmets without men. Who could ever have left so much behind? Certainly not the living.

Moving away from the crest, we hiked inland a short distance and took up positions along a hedgerow. I thought about how American and Allied forces left the English coast in thousands of ships and aircraft and stormed five beaches here in Normandy in a massive assault to push the Germans back. Paratroopers were the vanguard, and though many were killed or drowned, their objectives were successful.

Eventually my reverie faded and I returned to the present to find that I was beginning to dry out, and my feet weren't stinging as much now. We rested here, protected by hedgerows, for a couple of days before being split up and sent to units under fire. We were part of the 1st Army under the command of General Bradley, just numbers now, no names: all destined to become infantry replacements. I was a highly trained infantry soldier headed for the front, and my extensive training, along with some luck, would get me through the war alive, but I didn't know it then. In spite of all that I had done in the last two years, I knew this was only the beginning.

* * * * *

I wouldn't learn until much later that my good buddy, George Vath, died on this beach on D-Day. He was with the 1st Division. When the war ended I went to his home expecting a joyous reunion; instead, I was met at the front door by his mother. Her face bore her burden as she softly spoke of her son's death. George had been stuck by artillery and killed instantly. I felt deeply saddened for her loss and the loss of my friend George. Very much like life itself, our friendship was brief but meaningful. I would come to learn many times over that life is fleeting. It can be snuffed out in a moment's notice or without any notice at all.

19
99th Infantry Battalion (Separate)
Company D

The Army was always asking for volunteers, and today was no different. Today's request wasn't the usual counting out the first ten or twenty guys in a line, not this time. I knew there was an element of danger by the way we were asked. "I need a few men; step forward if you want to volunteer," a lieutenant said to us. Knowing damned well that I'd be sent to the front, I volunteered anyway, but only a few others joined me. Waiting was difficult for me; I wanted to move on. We were to be taken immediately to our new unit, the 99th Infantry Battalion (Separate), as infantry replacements, so we grabbed our gear and left our temporary camp in the hedgerows that same afternoon and arrived at our new destination sometime during the night.

The 99th was cleaning up in Cherbourg, had suffered some losses, and needed a few replacements. Upon our arrival, we were immediately taken into a basement or underground headquarters lit only by candlelight. The men inside were speaking a language that was foreign to me, although I knew it wasn't German. The whole scene had an air of mystery to it and I wondered what the hell was going on.

Speaking to me in English, a tall, sandy-haired man approached me, pulled out a chair and gestured for me to sit down. He then settled into his own chair and began to question me about my knowledge of infantry weapons. He treated me with a great deal of respect, like I was someone special, even offering me a cigarette. When I told him that I was qualified on machine guns, mortar guns, and any infantry weapon, he traded my rifle for a .45 caliber pistol and some hand grenades. I was taken immediately to Company D, a mortar section.

I soon learned that the men of the 99th were speaking Norwegian! I had volunteered myself into a Norwegian outfit, a bunch of really great guys. The men in Company D were happy to have me, and they let me know it. I felt satisfied with my new unit and sensed there was something very special about it. I was pleased to finally have an assignment, especially on the mortars. Mortar and machine gun sections had a lot more fire power than a rifle company. In the months ahead, however, I would discover that these were dangerous places to be, and certainly not the most coveted jobs, but I was very familiar with these weapons and the assignment would provide the challenge I desired.

MAPS AND
PHOTOGRAPHS

Map of Western Europe by R. S. Wagner.

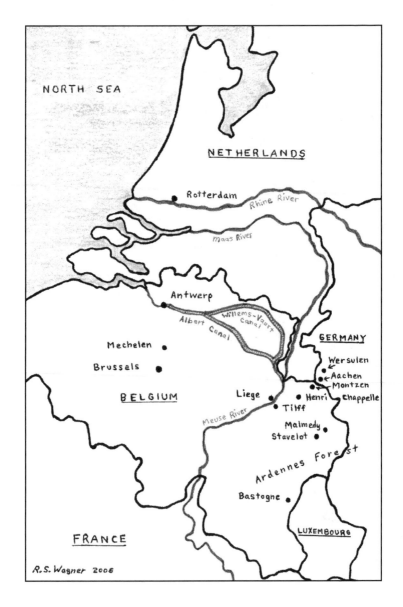

Map of Belgium and the Netherlands by R. S. Wagner.

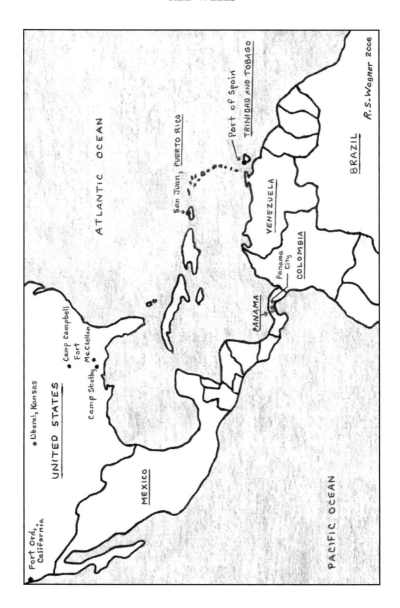

Map of the United States and the Caribbean by R. S. Wagner.

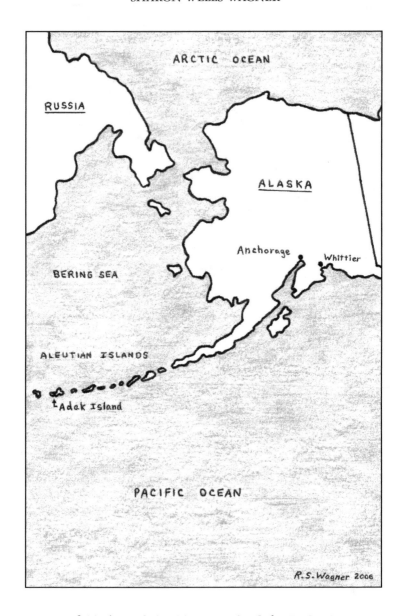

Map of Alaska and the Aleutian Islands by R. S. Wagner.

Red Wells, age 11, wearing knickers.

Red Wells, age 12, (right) with Sonny, holding toy gun.

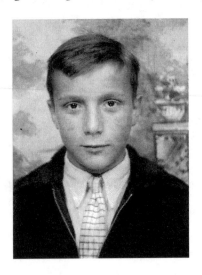

Red Wells, age 13, dressed for school.

At the Hope Rescue Mission in Reading, Red Wells got a meal and a bed for the night for the price of a prayer.

Red Wells, age 17, (right) fishing with Willie Weller.[1]

Pvt. Red Wells, age 18, in Panama.[1]

Pfc. Red Wells at Dockside Camp in Port of Spain, Trinidad.

Red Wells (left) and his buddy, George "Bud" Vath, at Camp
Shelby, Mississippi.

Red Wells (right) and cousin, Albert Hoffman, at home for an
11-day leave before shipping to Europe.

A few men from the 99th Infantry Battalion (Separate).[2]

Medic Marvin Skogrand (left) and Pfc Joseph Hoffland.[3]

One of my buddies, fellow mortar gunner Arne Oustad.[4]

Men of the 99th Infantry Battalion (Separate) advancing on downtown Eisden, Belgium.[2]

Prisoner of War camp in Barneville, France.[5]

During the Bulge, the Army Air Corps mistakenly bombed Malmady while it was occupied by the 99th.[6]

This old mill at Masta, Belgium was the last position the 99th held during the Battle of the Bulge.[7]

A resort in Barneville, on the coast of France, occupied by
Company D.[7]

The newly formed 474th Infantry Regiment (Separate) on the
move into Germany from Barneville, France.[5]

Castle Thurn in Heroldsbach, Germany; Company D stayed here briefly before going into Regenstauf.[7]

Civilians in Germany during the war.

Red Wells (left) in Germany with Sgt. Arthur Fredricksen of
Company D.

Red Wells (right) with Lee Gardner of Company D.

Some of the guns gathered while disarming the German population.[6]

Nuremberg in ruins.[6]

The 474th traveled from LeHarve, France, to Oslo, Norway, on these LSTs.[6]

The 99th's housing while in Smestad, Norway.[6]

The 99th marches in the Honor Guard Parade in Oslo.
Thousands stood for hours in the rain to see their king.[3]

The 99th parades for King Haakon VII, Crown Prince Olav, and General Omar Bradley on Allied Forces Day.[3]

The American soldier had his day as the people of Norway celebrated the American 4th of July holiday.[3]

Red Wells often rode the horses in Smestad.

Jarvis Taylor on his way to guard a German installation.[7]

L to R: Sgt. Andrew Hoiem, Clarence Becker, Elies Popejoy,
and Ordean Halla on M8 armored vehicle.[7]

Yeanni and Bjorg, two young ladies I met in Norway.

Jarvis Taylor (left) and Kenneth Raby saying goodbye in Smestad.[7]

The 99th leaves Norway on the Bienville and heads for the States.[6]

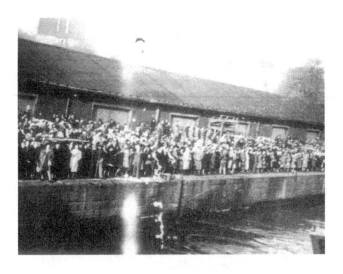

Enormous crowd gathers on the dock in Oslo to say goodbye to the 99th Infantry Battalion (Sep).[6]

Red Wells, military police, (left) and fellow MP at Camp
Campbell, Kentucky.[1]

Aerial view of Fort Ord, California.

Drill Instructor Red Wells, with recruits at Fort Ord.[1]

Physical fitness training for recruits at Fort Ord.

Recruits training on machine guns at Fort Ord.

D.I. Red Wells after a day of training recruits.[1]

An interesting photo by avid photographer, Red Wells.

Tallest and smallest recruits. Photo by Red Wells.

Model A Ford Red Wells purchased for $25.00.

Red Wells performed here at the Million Dollar Service Club.

Scenic Monterey Bay where Red Wells motored, fished, and spotted an occasional submarine.

Red Wells, rifleman (left), at a military funeral.

View across tundra on Adak, Aleutian Islands, Alaska.

Red Wells, of Task Force Williwaw, in front of his Quonset
hut in Adak.

Red Wells showing off his 80-lb pack.

Red Wells (center front) and task force members.

Celebrating Christmas on Adak. Willie, the tank driver, (right).

A few of the guys with one of the weasels on Adak.

Eva Roland Brice, mother of Red Wells.

Red Wells' sister, Betty, and her husband, Jack McCloskey.

Red Wells' brother, John Wells and his bride, Beatrice Arnold Wells.[8]

John Wells joins the Navy.[8]

Willie Weller, Red Wells' buddy in the CCCs, later became
Red's brother-in-law.[1]

Lifelong friend, Martha Erb, fed Red Wells when he was a
boy running the streets.

Lifelong friend, Anne Swink, grew up in an orphanage.

Helen Weller, age 3, future wife of Red Wells.

Helen Weller, age 13, when she only had eyes for Red Wells.

Red Wells' beautiful Helen when they began dating.[1]

Helen Weller and Red Wells both loved to fish.

Red Wells and grandson, Steve Wagner, in matching caps.
Steve is the author's son.

Red Wells and granddaughter, Stephanie Wagner, attired to win first place. Stephanie is the author's daughter.

Red Wells' favorite pastime is fishing.

Red Wells and grandson, Steve Wagner, with Steve's catch-of-
the day, a two and one-half pound rainbow trout.

Red Wells and granddaughter, Stephanie Wagner, smiling
over their successful catch of rainbow trout.

Four generations (L to R): Red Wells' wife Helen;
granddaughter, Shannon Illiano; daughter, Helen Wells
Stephenson; and great-granddaughter Alexandrea Illiano.[1]

Red Wells' wife, Helen, celebrating her and Red's 40th
wedding anniversary with their daughter, author, Sharon
Wells Wagner.

Red Wells at the World War II Memorial Dedication in
Washington, D.C. in May of 2004.

PART THREE

20
Eleven Months in Combat

Vitally important events over the next eleven months, from June 29, 1944 to May 8, 1945, would change my life forever. Nearly a year of combat would alter me as a person and fill my head with memories that would last a lifetime. I would become two different people, both filled with sadness and remorse—at times a person of great compassion for the devastation and horror I would witness, and at times a killer snuffing out countless lives without a thought. The memories would never go away, but time has a blessed way of easing pain, and that alone is what would make my gradual transition to civilian life possible.

The events of which I speak are described in the following chapters. They are primarily a chronicle, a historical account of my participation in the war in Europe. I have regaled you with only a few anecdotes, against the advice of a good editor. He had hoped to see a lot more. In spite of the fact that I have an excellent memory, there is very little with which to entertain you, only devastation, depression, and death, and it is not my wish to describe to you in graphic detail the horrors of war.

We, the 99th Infantry Battalion (Separate), were extremely busy during those eleven months, working long days, most often into long, lonely nights, sleeping very little, usually only a few hours at a time, busier and more exhausted than any of us would ever be again in our lives. What little free time we had was spent together eating, smoking cigarettes, and talking about families and friends and home. We were often split up and sent out on separate missions, but always came back together again, though the numbers were fewer each time. As the months progressed, we regularly lost men. Those were our most difficult days. We celebrated each day's survival with a cigarette, a pat on the back, and a chat with our buddies, and mourned each day's losses in silence.

The business of war was a round-the-clock job that included very little pleasure. I never played cards, saw a USO show, or had any kind of entertainment whatsoever, with the exception of an occasional radio broadcast from Axis Sally, if you consider enemy propaganda entertaining. The pleasure came to us in the form of a Christmas service in a hayloft in war-torn Malmady during the Bulge; or holding a smiling child in our arms in a liberated Paris; and later after the war ended, walking freely in the streets of Germany without fear of being killed by artillery or a sniper. These are the stories I've told.

The onset of WWII destroyed order and organization in much of Europe, took control of our lives, and filled us with fear and foreboding. We all learned from experience that war is a frightening and lonely business, especially when the world seems out of control. Lonely for those loved ones left behind at home and lonely for the fighting men on the front lines.

The men of the 99th were my buddies, each and every one of them, and we looked out for each other every day. We covered each other's backs in a fight, slept huddled together in foxholes when it was bitterly cold, and carried each other's bodies to safety when some were wounded or worse. Even in the darkest days of the war, we were never alone, we had each other. That was our only comfort, and that is what got us through it. War is a subject one cares not to remember, and wants even less to discuss. But because I've brought it up, I will endeavor to give you my best.

21

Cherbourg, France

The allied victory on D-Day gained us the beachheads of northern France, and a victory in Cherbourg would give us the peninsula, both necessary elements for a strong allied foothold in France. The battle for Cherbourg, under the command of General Bradley, was vital for the success of the French campaign. The Germans resisted fiercely under order by Hitler to hold the area at all costs. Besides being a tactical naval port, the city was home to German U-boats, and their defenders were not willing to lose these crucial assets.

After six days of intense fighting, the Germans, despite fierce determination, could not hold out any longer and surrendered on the 27th of June. By retaking the peninsula, the Allies had secured a vital deep water port for use by incoming supply and troop ships.

The 99th arrived in Cherbourg the day after it was retaken. The dead remained in the streets, lying where they fell. One young soldier, leaning upright against a door frame, looked like he might light up a cigarette any moment, except there was no breath left in his body. The carnage, mostly young German soldiers and some civilians, was vast and gruesome and seemed surreal to me, so I ignored it, looked past it, and went about my business, especially since I was not one of the men assigned to clean it up.

The citizens of Cherbourg, though not very friendly to Americans, came slowly out of hiding. Told by the German Army that we would kill them, they were terrified of us. Their heads had been filled with all kinds of propaganda. The residents were free to go about their business unless they interfered with our searches. Our job was to clean out any remaining Germans holed up in the city, patrol and guard military installations and acquisitions, and most important, hold the city.

We spread out all over town and rounded up or killed any remaining enemy; the choice was theirs. If their hands went into the air, they were treated humanely and taken to a POW camp for the remainder of the war where they'd be better fed than the rest of us. After two more days of continuous artillery bombardment, the forts in the bay were retaken as well. The Germans who survived the deluge hung white flags from the windows of the forts, and a few members of our battalion went over to accept the surrender. It would be some time before we could make use of the facilities because the Germans had deliberately destroyed the port when they knew they were losing the city. The vital Cherbourg peninsula, however, was now in the hands of the Allies

Cherbourg was the first time I was involved in any kind of combat. The resistance we encountered came mostly from snipers. I remember being shot at for the first time, an unfamiliar snapping sound coming towards me, and I didn't like it one bit. Fortunately my assailant had poor aim, but his efforts brought about his own demise when one of the men picked up on his position and dropped him quickly. Snipers were a problem in Cherbourg, and I would dread them all through the war. You never knew when you might get a bullet in the head.

Having been together since their training in the States, the 99th was a brotherhood, a tight bunch of guys working and fighting closely together, always covering each other's backs. They took care of their own; me included, as I witnessed today, and suffered greatly when one was lost. I was one of them now, one of the youngest, in fact, and they'd taken me under their wing. I was damn lucky.

22

The Clean Up Begins

We stayed in Cherbourg nearly two weeks until our objectives were completed, then moved out around the 9th of July and headed south for the front lines only a few short miles away. Because the Allies were pushing the Germans back steadily, our area of control grew larger and larger each day, until we eventually held the entire peninsula, clear down to St. Lo. We were constantly cleaning up pockets of resistance, mostly snipers, patrolling retaken territory round the clock, and confiscating abandoned weapons and ammunition, and anything else of worth left behind by the retreating Germans. We also picked up some prisoners along the way.

Cleaning up is a term generally used for the dangerous business of removing the enemy left behind, holed up in houses or buildings, although we found them everywhere: in trees, ditches, church steeples, you name it. The places one could hide were endless. There were always stragglers left behind in cities and villages that had been bombed or lobbed by artillery, and they were usually desperate, tired and hungry, and always dangerous. They'd hit us with machine gun fire or whatever they had left, but often ended up dying in the process. Of course, we suffered casualties as well.

We threw everything we had at them, especially automatic weapons, barging into homes peppering everything in front of us with machine gun fire. Sometimes I'd sneak up close and toss a grenade into a doorway or window if I could get close enough without getting shot first. The explosions were devastating and usually took care of the problem. When the dust settled I'd go cautiously inside to make sure the job was done. Most of the time I found a dead man; occasionally I found one severely wounded who I left to his fate and moved on with my squad, careful to put the memory of his face out of my mind

Somewhere south of Cherbourg I remember throwing a grenade into the window of a house that harbored one perpetrator. After the grenade exploded, a badly wounded German soldier stumbled out of the house and dropped to his knees in the street. The fear I witnessed in the eyes of that young man as he attempted too late to surrender, reminded me that war was a horrific waste of decent human beings. He collapsed and died almost immediately. Relieved, I moved on with my squad, glad that I didn't have to deal with him any further. It was much easier to look a dead man in the eyes than one you'd just wounded.

We took some prisoners during these crucial early days of the war, but mostly we killed a lot of people. I remember thinking that it all seemed very confusing to me at the time. There was a great urgency about getting the enemy; kill them or capture them, whatever it took, just get the job done. We had license to kill without limits or boundaries. "Go kill those Jerries," I remember one of our Sergeants telling us more than once. It was absolutely insane. I'd never been in combat before, so I resigned myself to the fact that this is what war must be like.

Ferreting out these stragglers was hazardous and difficult work. The searches, filled with many tense moments, seemed endless. There was so much ground to cover and we were constantly on the move. I was always keenly aware of my surroundings, carefully absorbing sights and sounds like the prey I might become. But I was the predator, by choice, and my fierce desire to survive turned me into a sly, swift killer achieving my objectives quickly. My years of jungle warfare training had taught me to become invisible when dealing with the enemy, and I'm certain that training saved my life more than once. Much later on, as the war wound down, more and more Germans surrendered to us, but not here or now. There was a lot of cleaning up to do; we would be very busy in the months ahead.

We bivouacked at Hau de Haut and began training for battles to come. We were taught how to set up roadblocks and also learned a good deal about hedgerow fighting—tactics that would prove necessary in the weeks to come. Setting up roadblocks involved a lot more than blocking a road with obstacles; it primarily involved strategies for holding back the enemy. We joined up with a Ranger group for a few weeks, and we all trained together, honing our skills even further.

About this time our battalion experienced its first air assault. Traveling at night by truck to meet up with the 2nd Armored Division, we were hit from the air. First came the flares that illuminated our position, then bombs began exploding all around us. German planes repeatedly strafed us with machine gun fire as well. Everyone dove for cover and, miraculously, the entire Battalion emerged unscathed. Although the Germans did not succeed in their mission to annihilate us, their sneak attack on our convoy scared the hell out of every one of us. After a couple days' travel by truck, we located and became attached to the 2nd Armored Division, and soon earned a reputation as the only battalion that the 2nd Armored Division had trouble keeping up with.

By late August the battalion was busy setting up roadblocks. Unfortunately this usually involved a skirmish. We set up our equipment and weapons, dug ourselves in, and blasted any enemy soldiers or vehicles attempting to pass. No one ever got through any of our roadblocks. German tanks were generally impenetrable, but we stopped them by blowing up the treads with bazookas. One or two rounds from a bazooka usually did the trick. They were shoulder-mounted, mid-range weapons that fired very explosive and destructive rockets. We also used them to stop any armored vehicles that we couldn't stop with our machine gun or mortar fire.

The French countryside with its fields and hedgerows slowed us down somewhat. There were thousands of fields surrounded by hedgerows, mounds of earth, four feet high and just as thick, dating back to the Romans, when farmers first began outlining their fields. Narrow lanes ran between the hedgerows. To make matters worse, trees and vines and thorny shrubs grew out of them, and the roots made it nearly impossible to break through the boscage. Vehicles, even tanks, could not drive through them. A tank attempting to climb a hedgerow risked drawing anti-tank fire at its vulnerable underside. If a tank became disabled, it blocked the lane so others could not pass. Men had great difficulty getting over the hedgerows, as well, and rarely tried. Fortunately, there were openings randomly in the mounds, which we utilized cautiously.

Normandy, with its thousands of fields and hedgerows, provided natural fortification for the Germans. The hedgerows made excellent places for them to hide, making our work more difficult, so we proceeded quietly and with great deal of caution. There were often mines along the tops of the hedgerows, planted there deliberately. This was a fairly common tactic and often proved deadly to the Allies.

The men split up into small rifle groups, supported by a mortar or machine gun, and worked their way slowly and quietly down the lanes between the rows and across the fields. I was usually on the mortars, often carrying the base plate, a large thick steel plate on which we could quickly mount our mortar gun. The plate was heavy, maybe 40 pounds, and I usually carried it in front of my body for a little extra protection where it actually took a few hits. There were times when we were suddenly attacked and had to dive for cover and stay down, and I'd prop that plate in front of my body.

Our squad was crossing a field early one morning when we heard cries coming from a shallow ditch just ahead of us. Approaching cautiously, we found a German soldier who had been left behind by his unit. His cry for help sounded like that of a boy, and when I approached him I realized he was not much older than a boy, seventeen, maybe eighteen. His right leg was completely gone, blown off by artillery most likely, and he was bleeding profusely. Two of our men, one a medic, approached the wounded man cautiously and applied a tourniquet to what was left of his mangled limb. The rest of us looked on in silence, completely tuned to our surroundings, yet engrossed by the scene unfolding before us—two men giving aid and comfort, not to the enemy, but to a fellow human being.

Knowing he wouldn't last very long, we left the young man to his fate and moved on. We had a lot of ground to cover.

Moving on foot and hunting the enemy this way was a painfully slow and stressful process. I remember getting so close to Germans at times that we could hear them whispering just on the other side of the mound. It was very risky, and we had a few casualties, but those hedgerows were clean as a whistle when we finished with them. Holding ground that had been retaken by the Allies and cleaning up as we moved forward was exhausting. I often wondered how we kept up the pace.

23
Elbeuf, France

Near the end of August, we reached the perimeter of Elbeuf. Our approach was met with resistance in the form of artillery being lobbed in our direction, and I had a feeling what lay ahead was going to be difficult and costly. The Germans were just ahead of us, holed up in town and dug in tight. We were told that we'd probably encounter trouble because Elbeuf was strategically important to the Germans. It provided an escape route into Normandy via the Seine River. Our tanks couldn't get past disabled German tanks that littered the bridge into town, so we went in without backup.

Our only approach into town, which was located in a valley, was down a steep hill that provided no cover for us. Machine gunners established their positions to cover the rifle companies that had spread out in the streets. I was on the mortars, which we set up on a hill facing town. I began feeding shells into the tube, one after the other, in a non-stop barrage of fire. Their mortar shells and screaming meemies were exploding all around us, spraying deadly shrapnel in every direction. Because the shelling was so intense, we were ordered to fire white phosphorous to drive out those Germans on the mortars. The phosphorous worked quickly, disabling the mortar and rocket fire, and sent Germans running for their lives, the phosphorous painfully burning their skin. Then they started firing their deadly 88s at us and pinned our rifle companies down in the streets.

Being in the throes of battle was both stimulating and terrifying. Stimulating when I had the advantage, when I was in control lobbing mortar shells one after another at those bastards, killing them off without a thought; but terrifying when I was outnumbered, or short of ammunition, or unable to fire the mortars because I was dug in, hiding from deadly 88 flak or artillery, or faced with the realization that my buddies were dead or seriously wounded next to me and I couldn't do a damned thing about it. This was the case in Elbeuf; we were attacked viciously that first day but fought back hard and, by some miracle, took Elbeuf before day's end.

After securing the town, we took some prisoners and locked them in a courtyard for the night. Then we settled down, exhausted, taking turns getting a little shut-eye, and keeping a watchful eye on our perimeters while holding down the fort. By mid-morning the next day, the tide had changed and the Germans surprised us by lobbing 88s and artillery at us from across the river. I never saw men dig in so fast. I made a beeline for my mortar gun and jumped head first into the hole we'd dug out the day before. Not all of my buddies made it back to the hole, so we were a couple of guys short. The man next to me got hit in the helmet with 88 flak, but was not injured. As it turned out, my whole squad survived the assault without injury, but I'll never forget how they hit us suddenly and brutally, pinning us down. No one could move without becoming a target.

Some of our men were wounded and a few were killed, including officers who were in our command post when it was hit. By early evening armored reinforcements arrived to help get us out of our dangerous predicament, blasting the hell out of the Germans across the river. Under heavy fire, we made a precarious ascent up the same steep hill that brought us here and headed back to our bivouac area. Luck was with us on this mission, at least with those of us who survived.

The German 88 was the weapon I dreaded most during the war, regardless of how it was used. It was originally an anti-aircraft weapon but was found to be particularly effective against infantry and ground armor. It fired a high velocity flak shell which burst into a large cloud of deadly shrapnel. Later in the war, the Germans used them as anti-tank weapons, and mounted them on their own Tiger and Nashorn tanks and others, firing them at men on the ground and at tanks. Their effect on the battlefield was unmistakable, as their fierce rate of fire and high muzzle velocity made them swift killers.

I remember having 88s fired directly at us from a very short distance. I'd seen men get hit with flak from 88s; their bodies were no longer recognizable. Fortunately, we were well dug in and miraculously survived the air bursts above our heads. Some of the guys were wounded by shrapnel, I wasn't, but we had some close calls. 88s were often mounted on tanks and easy to spot. We could see them coming around a corner, and as the turret moved slowly in our direction, we knew we had only seconds to get the hell out of the way. Once aimed, it was too late to escape. We could identify 88s by their sound. They had a distinctly frightening sound, a reverberating BOOM BOOM upon firing and exploding. The shell from an

88 hit its target almost immediately because it traveled at such a high rate of speed.

The first time I ever heard screaming meemies was on our approach to Elbeuf. They were explosive rocket-like shells that whistled like fireworks, only much louder, and screamed horribly, sounding like they were tumbling and twirling erratically, making one think the shells were out of control and could strike anywhere. I found them to be mostly annoying, meant to harass more than anything else, but some of the guys were really bothered by the sound of them. They were meant to terrify more than destroy, and I could see the fear in the faces of some of the guys whenever the screaming meemies starting coming in.

As we continued our move through France towards Belgium and Holland, we slept anywhere we could, mostly on the ground, but a bombed-out house or basement provided a sense of comfort and security after so much fighting. We were exhausted and rested when we could, but the sounds of war were ever present, even at night. No matter what shred of solitude we managed to find in the basement of a house or a foxhole, the sounds of war were not far off. Explosions, gunfire, vehicles, the wail of human distress—their echoes drifted in from the darkness and reminded us that we were in the middle of something vast and ugly. And the smell—even a moment of reverie couldn't mask the smell. It lingered everywhere and hung like a fog and reeked of gasoline and corpses, of burning wood and metal. It stuck to our clothes and haunted every waking moment.

The only real comfort we had was knowing that we were not alone—we had each other. On break the men shared stories of home and often their last cigarettes. That's how we lived. We suffered such things as best we could. In the twilight hours of those European nights, the sounds and smells of war were omnipresent reminders that we were far from home.

All through the war I witnessed a great deal of devastation, the most shocking of which were the horrors suffered by civilians. Many tens of thousands were killed, but the ones who suffered most were the ones left behind by the war as it moved constantly forward. Many of them were women and children who had no means of escaping the Allies' deluge of bombing upon their homes and villages to rid them of the scourge of German occupation. Even though leaflets dropped on their villages warned them of the upcoming barrage, many of them stayed, hiding in the basements of their homes, because they had no means of fleeing to safety.

I witnessed over and over the sounds of grief emanating from desperate souls wounded or frantically searching for loved ones amid the rubble and devastation of their homes and lives. I could offer them no solace; I had none to give. I was faced with the dangers of ridding what was left of their villages of snipers and collaborators.

The greatest pain I suffered during the war was not my own hunger, cold, or physical discomfort, or even remorse for the many men whose lives I had taken, but the depth of human sadness in the eyes of women and children and old men. That was the greatest pain of all.

24
Canal Drive
Belgium & Holland

After the fighting at Elbeuf, we were given a few days of much needed rest, but it was all too brief and we were soon back in business. During this time we moved forward constantly, patrolling, hunting down, and cleaning up Germans in hiding. Sometimes a few, and sometimes many, like in Elbeuf. The people in Belgium were not afraid to share any information on the position of enemy soldiers and breathed a sigh of relief as we cleaned out leftover Germans from one village after another. We were extremely careful, covering each other's backs constantly. There were many villages to search and roadblocks to set up. It seemed an endless task.

I was dug in with my mortar squad one morning, holding a position to defend a roadblock that my Company had just established, when two Belgian men sporting white arm bands approached me and said in broken English, "We have spotted Germans on a ridge two miles southeast of your roadblock. They have two tanks and about forty men." The information they gave me confirmed our own suspicions, and as usual, we were prepared. Those Jerries would not survive the day.

The tattered white fabric knotted snuggly around their upper arms identified the two men as members of the Belgian

Underground. Reporting the whereabouts of enemy in the area was a common practice of the Underground. Poorly dressed and struggling to survive in their war ravaged country, these very ordinary people were proud and courageous, risking their lives to bring information to the Allies. "Many thanks," I told them as I shook each man's hand in gratitude.

It was here in Belgium where I observed human beings taking into their own hands the fate of those who'd betrayed their country. Collaborators, those men and women who had cooperated with the Germans, regardless of reason, were dealt with harshly. I often witnessed men and women digging their own graves, sometimes just one large pit, then being shot to death by members of the Belgian Underground, and occasionally by ordinary citizens. Women were shamed first by cutting off their hair, sometimes made to dance around in a circle, then shot in the head.

The men meant nothing to me. I cared less about their crimes and felt that they were traitors to their own country. But the woman I often felt sorry for because many of them were young and had children at home. But that didn't matter now because they'd associated themselves with the enemy, often at the threat of having their own families harmed. They were dead either way: at the hands of the Germans if they didn't cooperate, or at the hands of their own countrymen if they did. As a witness to these atrocities I had to keep reminding myself that this was war, and the world would not always seem out of control.

In a small town in Belgium I was conducting searches with a squad of men. The sun had dipped below the horizon, darkness was rapidly settling in, and the men were exhausted. During one of our searches of an abandoned house earlier in the day, we found a large feather bed in an upstairs room. The house had sustained minor damage but stood intact in spite of the devastation around it, and would make a fine refuge for my squad. We wasted no time in settling in for the night. Four of us made a beeline for the bed, and the remaining few guys bedded down on the floor.

Crowded as we were with four men lying crossways on the bed, the pure comfort of the down-filled ticking beneath our tired bodies eased us into a blissful repose. The weight of four men in one bed caused it to sag somewhat and our bodies began to roll slowly towards the center until we were bumped up tight against each other like kippers in a can. My buddies Clarence, Olaf, and Arne were already asleep and didn't notice. I was wedged in between two of them, but I didn't care. I felt happy and secure because I wasn't alone. Before drifting off, I looked at the face of my buddy next to me and imagined this is what it must feel like to have a big brother to climb into bed with when you're scared. And we'd been scared a lot lately, but not tonight. Tonight was special; we had a feather bed!

Hours into our slumber, my keen sense of hearing awakened me to the sound of mortar shells being fired from a tube. There was no mistaking the familiar booming and whistling sounds of incoming fire. Just seconds after waking up, a huge explosion blew away a large section of the roof over our heads. Myriad stars in the clear night sky were suddenly visible through the gaping hole, but I never noticed as I protected my head with my arms against debris that rained down all over us. We got out of that feather bed even faster than we got in, ran for our lives, and never looked back. Fortunately, no one was injured.

By mid-September, we bivouacked outside of Mechelen, Belgium, near Holland, to reconnoiter the area for German activity. Patrols reported back that the area north of Maastricht, near the Willems Vaart Canal in Holland was crawling with Germans, so we knew what lay ahead for us. Those Jerries were dug in, but we were going to get them.

Before beginning our assault against so many Germans, the 2nd Armored Division softened things up for us with a deluge of artillery. As they fired over our heads, I watched the shells flying through the air and exploding all over the island. When the 2nd Armored lifted its fire, we were ordered to move out across what was left of the bridge blown up earlier by the Germans. Because 88s were still coming at us heavy, our first couple of attempts to storm the island failed. Still under intense fire, and against impossible odds, one of our guys bolted for the bridge, and the rest of us followed. I remember leaping across damaged and missing girders and stepping over bodies as I ran for my life, like a deer in a field of hunters. Unbelievably, not a single man was hit. We should all have died on that bridge; I'll never understand why we didn't.

By some miracle, we all survived the dash across the bridge, but would not be so fortunate over the next few days. Even though the Germans had the advantage of being dug in, our artillery had pushed them back, leaving empty fox holes and trenches into which we rapidly dove for cover. The only Germans remaining were dead ones. We rolled their bodies out of the holes and used them for cover.

We had carried machine guns with us but weren't able to set them up until darkness fell, giving us some blessed cover.

Artillery fire had forced the Germans to take cover behind a high stone wall that divided the island. Well fortified, they had us pinned down now, struggling but determined to hold our ground until dark when we would set up machine guns around our perimeter and push them back. The night air was cool, and because my clothing was wet, I was damned cold.

Being pinned down, or trapped like we were here, in spite of our fear, enhanced our instincts and made us more dangerous. The thought that we were trapped and could perish before the next sunrise never crossed my mind. Survival was paramount, but so was allegiance. There was a comradery among us, a fellowship unlike any I had ever known; and we looked out for each other all the time. Today would be no different. Perhaps this is what defines courage, not the lack of human fear, but the willingness to rise above it. And we would rise above it. We had been pinned down before, and I knew we'd be pinned down again before this war would end.

I was reminded that men are inevitably lost in war when I heard voices futilely calling out for a medic. I could see my buddy, Clarence, huddled in a hole nearby. He was a replacement who joined the battalion as an infantry soldier some time after I did. I came to know him when he became our aid man. He decided early on that he wasn't cut out to carry a gun, so he became a medic, and a good one at that. He had heard the cries for help, too, but didn't make a move. No one made a move. I laid there wondering what I would have done had I been a medic, quickly coming to the conclusion that because I was impulsive, I'd have ended up a dead man.

I remember feeling scared for Clarence, afraid that he might get himself shot. He was my buddy, one of many, and getting himself killed would have devastated me. In spite of the fact that the cries for help continued, I felt relieved that he and the others stayed put.

The Germans had killed a few of our medics recently and we knew they were just waiting to pick off some more. The red crosses painted on the helmets of unarmed men where supposed to exempt them from danger, but sadly set them apart as targets instead. Because the fighting at the canal was so intense, Clarence knew it would have been suicide to make a move, so he and the other aid men made the sadder but wiser choice.

We took turns on the machine guns round the clock in a continuous barrage of fire. On a break, exhausted, I crawled on my belly through the darkness into a small trench behind me and curled up back to back against the form of a man who was already asleep. Resting this way provided comfort as well as warmth. Fog had begun to settle in and hovered low, shrouding the darkness in an opaque veil that limited our vision to within a few feet. The fog was eerie and the night ominous, but I quickly fell victim to the exhaustion I struggled with all day. When I was awakened a few hours later to take my turn on the guns, I realized my companion hadn't moved. It was daylight now and I shuddered at the realization that I had slept back to back with a dead German. That was the only time I ever slept with a German!

After three tense days, we killed enough Jerries to force them back, and I remember our battalion commander climbing up and standing on the massive stone wall, shouting and waving us over. We quickly scaled the wall, took cover, and assessed the situation. Finding no Germans in the immediate area, we came out of hiding, moved forward, and soon learned that the enemy had completely cleared out. After three days of intense fighting, we had retaken the island. With the exception of their dead lying all over the place, the Germans had retreated. Sadly, a few of our good men died at the Canal, and dozens were wounded.

After three days with nothing to eat except crackers, a D-bar, or whatever else we had in our pockets, we went into Belgium to a camp near Montzen to rest. Exhausted and hungry, we feasted on warm C-rations. Here we got cleaned up and refitted with new weapons and supplies. After two weeks of rest, our new orders arrived; we were going to Wersulen.

It was sometime during our two-week rest that Sergeant Kelly assigned me and a few other men to guard 1st Army Division Headquarters which was housed in a resort south of Spa, near Chaudfontaine and loaded with big brass. Many important meetings were taking place during the time I was on duty, and there was a sense of urgency about the activity there. Additional guards were spread out around the perimeter of the building, each of us heavily armed, with orders to "shoot to kill" anyone attempting to approach. My vantage point afforded me the opportunity to see General Bradley, General Montgomery, General Patton, and others up close. They frequently walked right by me. Patton, who was tall, stood out from the others because he was always meticulously dressed. He carried two ivory handled pistols and often wore cavalry boots.

I would have the opportunity to see Patton on several more occasions before the war ended. I saw him once in the turret of a Sherman tank in Belgium, out in front of his men, headed for the front lines. He always waved at us, and always greeted the men. We respected him enormously and would have followed him anywhere.

Guard duty was an interesting and welcome, though brief, respite from combat, and my time at 1st Army Division Headquarters passed quickly.

* * * * *

Clarence survived the Canal Drive and the war as well, and we remained friends for many years to come, but he carried with him a terrible guilt for not coming to the aid of those men during the canal drive. Let it be known, however, that Clarence and our other medics helped save lives throughout the remainder of the war. We were all faced with many difficult decisions during the war; sometimes lives could be saved and sometimes not.

25

Battle for Aachen

The battle for Aachen was in full swing. We were dug in on the edge of town, near Wersulen, blocking the enemy's only means of escape, the main highway between Wersulen and Aachen. The Germans were well fortified, heavily armed, and unyielding. We had them trapped; they had us pinned down.

Frequent rains soaked our clothing, and the autumn nights in Europe were damn cold. During the entire European campaign I had no scarf or gloves, only an Army-issued raincoat that absorbed water nearly as well as a sponge. The Red Cross handed out gloves and other small necessities to men in larger units on the front lines, but encounters with the Red Cross by smaller units like ours were rare.

We often had little or no food during combat, subsisting on whatever was left in our pockets. Usually if one man had no food, then none of us had any. But any morsels we had were shared, cigarettes included. Because we were often pinned down, we went for days with nothing to eat. And don't forget, the Germans were shooting at us most of the time, along with a constant barrage of artillery; incoming mail, we called it. Under these circumstances it was almost impossible to get supplies to us. This was the case here in Aachen.

The wait for orders to take Aachen was an agonizing couple of days. Stress during combat was one thing, but the stress of anticipating it was worse. Waiting to strike allowed my mind too much free time to wander, filling my head with dark and dismal thoughts. During combat, I had no time to think about dying, getting wounded or being captured; I was too busy staying focused on the job at hand.

My survival instinct was strong. Staying alive meant the success of the mission, and I lived for that alone. I just kept fighting, moving forward, digging and firing until the job was done, and so did everyone around me. But when I returned, battered and exhausted, for a couple of days rest before my next assignment, I wondered if I could ever be human again; I hated the machine that I had become. It frightened me.

Finally, on October 16, our orders came and, prepared for the worst, we moved towards Aachen under artillery fire. The 30th Division and the 1st Division had Aachen surrounded except for the main highway between there and Wersulen. We dug in by the road and held back the Germans for nine long days, literally using our bodies as shields, trapping them in town.

The Germans had a sizable force of artillery nearby and, determined to hold onto this route, bombarded us continuously. Screaming meemies soared overhead and exploded all around us. The many buildings in town provided perfect cover for enemy tanks and artillery, and in spite of the fact that the Germans had the advantage, we had them surrounded on all sides.

Our own Air Force bombed and strafed Aachen continuously, seeming to have little effect on the well fortified Germans. I was on the mortars; we fired in a relentless salvo, dodging grenades and air bursts from 88s the whole time. We endured intense, heavy fighting, day and night, for nine days straight, and became completely exhausted. Non-stop artillery and grenades exploding all around us made sleep nearly impossible. The air was cold, and rain fell continuously. Food and water were scarce, and I learned later that some of our men ran out of ammunition.

By some miracle we succeeded in holding back the enemy until infantry from the 30th Division arrived to take over. We lost a couple dozen men and fifty or so were wounded, a large toll for such a small battalion. Our wounded went with us, but because we had to get out quickly, our dead were left behind to be picked up later.

The Battle for Aachen was nine days of pure hell. Our small battalion, though outnumbered and outgunned, was brought in to help hold the city until reinforcements arrived to aid the 30th and First Divisions. Once again we were successful, and by pure determination survived another day. Even though we were given some replacements, our small battalion was growing smaller with each battle; however, our diminished size did not alter our determination. We were ready for whatever lay ahead.

Later we learned that the battle for Aachen was one of the heaviest concentrations of fire power against American troops since D-Day. I believe it. Only nine days; it seemed like ninety.

26
Tilff, Belgium

After the battle for Aachen, the battalion was physically and mentally battered and in dire need of rest, so we moved back into Belgium for a break. I believe we settled in somewhere near Henri-Chapelle, taking up residence in barns and other small buildings where we could sleep inside for a change. It was cold now, but we were fortunate to have shelter to settle into at night. It was each man to his own, but a lot more comfortable than a wet, muddy foxhole. We lived outdoors by day, keeping warm by campfire, and ate warm food for a change, usually C-rations. Food was available to us when our kitchen trucks were with us. In combat, however, that was a different story. After a brief rest, we were ordered to move to Tilff.

The move to Tilff was made around Thanksgiving, although I don't recall celebrating the holiday. We were here for a 'break.' Our breaks were a reprieve from combat only, but not from training, patrolling, and guard duty. Training honed our skills and increased our chances of staying alive. Patrolling was an absolute necessity all through the war; ground retaken from the enemy had to be constantly monitored. During this particular break we were told to be especially diligent in keeping a look out for infiltrators, German paratroopers in particular. Thus, we were split up into very small groups, eight or ten men, and spread far and wide in constant watch.

Breaks usually meant probably not getting shot at, but the possibility always existed, and this was most definitely the case here in Tilff. We knew the Germans were very close by, not necessarily within earshot, but still too close to let our guard down.

A few of our vehicles were equipped with military radios which were a source of occasional entertainment during a break. Some of my buddies from the mortar squads and I would tune in to Axis Sally. Her propaganda was meant to lower our spirits, but worked quite the opposite in that we found her amusing. Clarence, Harry, Arne and I, and a few other guys whose names I can't recall, would gather round the radio listening for the location of our own Battalion to be announced over the air waves. Although I never heard Axis Sally mention the 99th, she regularly made comments about other units and announced over the air their precise locations. "Good morning, Yankees of the 1st Division. I see that your unit is heading south today just 2 miles from Liege," she would say. "When you arrive, you will receive a warm welcome." Her so-called 'intelligence reports' always amazed us.

Her sultry voice was entertaining and I tried to imagine what she might look like. I was certain that she looked like a sexy blond starlet right out of a Hollywood movie, as I listened to the big band tunes she played, airing straight from Berlin. She also let us know that our wives were being 'taken care of' back home by our own buddies while we were off fighting a war.

As it turned out, Axis Sally wasn't a starlet after all. She was an ordinary American woman who had studied music in a college in Germany, and had fallen in love with and married her professor, a German. He later got her involved with radio, and that is how she became Axis Sally. When the war ended, however, she was brought back to the States, tried and convicted of treason, and sentenced to many years in prison.

Tilff is where I learned to fear buzz bombs. A few of the guys and I had a very close call one day when a V2 fell prematurely near Tilff. A bright light appeared to be falling down directly above me, and certain that it was a V2, I dove head first into in a hole, only seconds before the weapon struck less than 50 yards away. The explosion shook the ground violently, but the concussion passed over me because I was in a pretty deep hole. There were ditches, bomb craters and foxholes all over Europe, and miraculously I was within a few feet of one when I needed it most. Otherwise, I'd have been blown to bits. The bomb left a crater twenty feet deep, and a ringing in my ears for quite some time afterwards.

Liege, which was northeast of us, just a few miles away, was inundated with buzz bombs day and night. We didn't know it yet, but the Germans were about to break through the front lines into the Ardennes, and it was during this time that they picked up the pace on their assault of Liege. There was a constant barrage on Liege, terrorizing every civilian in the area. During the Ardennes offensive, nearly ninety buzz bombs struck there in a single day; the damage was beyond description. The constant assault of Liege created a lot of stress for the battalion, and the residents of Tilff, terrified of being hit, stayed mostly hidden. It was heartbreaking to see people living in fear like this, especially children.

I saw too many buzz bombs and the horrific devastation they brought with them. There were two kinds: V1s and V2s. V1s looked a lot like a small airplane, were not very fast, and could be shot down by aircraft. British Spitfires chased and shot down many of them over the English Channel. They were timed, made a buzzing sound, sometimes sputtered and fizzled while they ran out of fuel, and then fell straight down. These were used earlier in the war and were launched from coastal bases in the Netherlands, France, and Belgium by the Germans against England. I watched many pucker out and drop to the ground; some even changed direction in mid-air, turning around and going back the way they came. Most of the time a V1 just sputtered and continued on until it ran out of fuel, came to a standstill, and fell down and exploded.

Later on in the war, the V1 was replaced by the V2, which was launched from farther inland vertically from a stand. The V2 was a long range ballistic missile with fins, more accurate than the V1, but still indiscriminate in its ability to reach a target. The V2 was designed to be a weapon of terror, carried a one-ton warhead, could be fired hundreds of miles towards its target, and had the ability take out nearly an entire city block. Civilians were terrified of these bombs, and rightfully so. V2s, which were relatively silent, could be spotted at night due to the exhaust but were nearly invisible by day due to the high altitude from which they fell. Only a bright ball of light was visible seconds before a V2 hit its target. I know; it happened to me. The resulting explosions were completely devastating and tens of thousands of innocent people lost their lives.

27

Battle of the Bulge

The Battle of the Bulge, also known as the Ardennes offensive, or the Breakthrough, took place during the worst weather that Europe had seen in decades. Striving to slice the Allied line in two, Hitler made his last massive counteroffensive against the Allies. Proceeding against the advice of his own military advisors, Hitler succeeded in breaking through the Allied front lines into the Ardennes area of Belgium, a large densely wooded area, with his sights set on invading Antwerp. The Allies were caught off guard and lost a large section of territory to the Germans, but within a week thousands of reinforcements would arrive to repel Hitler's advance.

The Allies knew the Germans were low on fuel and felt this would dampen their ambitions and restrict their movements. However, they underestimated Hitler, never expecting he would break through the front line and go west through an area of dense forest during such bad weather. Snow fell constantly, the wind blew fiercely, and the bitter cold and poor visibility seemed a deterrent. Hitler, on the other hand, felt his presence in the Ardennes would be masked by the snow and fog which hung low, obscuring much of the landscape. He knew, too, that the Allies were heavily concentrated to the north and south, but not so much in this area. So early on the morning of the 16th of December, he attacked viciously. Hitler's plan was bold but foolish.

Terrible weather and German infiltrators prolonged the fighting through the New Year, and the real Allied counterattack did not begin until the third of January. Eager to eliminate the German salient in the center of their line, Patton and Montgomery agreed to move north and south, respectively, and encircle the enemy troops. When their forces finally met up on the 15th of January, the German advance was halted for good. It would be some time before the previous month's borders would be re-established, but for now the enemy was weakened considerably.

The Battle of the Bulge was essentially a last ditch effort by the Germans to break Allied hopes of taking Germany. Hitler wanted to drive a wedge between Roosevelt and Churchill, forcing some kind of peace with one or the other, in order to focus his efforts on the Eastern front. He knew that his days were numbered, and his only real hope was to shift his efforts into fighting one front at a time. He also hoped that by shaking things up in the west, he would be able to buy time to finish critical arms projects. But the unexpected rapid reactions by the Allies dashed his hopes, and he was left with the prospect of fighting a numerically superior force while his own production capabilities dwindled.

While Hitler was making plans to go west to Antwerp, we were settled in at Tilff keeping supply lines open and patrolling for German infiltrators when we got the word to move out. It was December 16th when we received priority orders to pack quickly and lightly, weapons, ammunition and combat gear only. Told that we would be gone for just a few days, most of us left dry socks, rations, and other necessities behind. I remember the urgency with which we were ordered to pack. "Light pack," we were told, "we're movin' out." Loaded into trucks and traveling mostly under cover of darkness, I suspected the worst. Anticipating what might come was often worse to me than fighting it out with the Germans. Combat kept me so damned busy that I had little time to be afraid. But I was anxious now as our convoy screeched to a halt in the early morning hours. It was nearly dawn, and we were in Malmady.

During our move to the Ardennes, we encountered American troops coming towards us, moving away from the Malmady area—retreating. They were confused and frightened; some had gotten separated from their units, but most were being pushed back by huge numbers of very aggressive and heavily armed Germans. The area was believed to be overrun by Germans but we kept moving forward anyway. We passed through allied roadblocks and were told to go back; "you guys are crazy," they told us, "you're gonna get yourselves killed." But we kept going; we had a job to do.

Expecting to find the Germans well ensconced in Malmady, we approached with caution, but arrived to find it quiet and deserted, except for residents who were hiding in cellars and shelters. We didn't feel welcome in this pro-Nazi town, especially since the Germans were just over the hill. We quickly dug ourselves in on the edge of town; I was up a hill on the mortars. A couple of other units arrived shortly afterwards, the 526th Armored Infantry Battalion and the 825th Tank Destroyer Battalion. Even with the help of these additional units, we were well outnumbered when the Germans arrived the next morning.

By daybreak the Germans began their assault, hitting us hard with American tanks and vehicles they had captured, their own Tigers, machine guns, and everything else they had in their arsenal. The fighting was fierce and vicious as they advanced inch by inch, getting precariously close to us, but, by some miracle, we held them back.

My time was spent dodging artillery and air bursts from 88s while feeding 81mm shells one after the other into a tube. We fired mortar shells non-stop. The Germans had more than a few 88s dug in that were creating serious problems for us, so under the direction of our Sergeant, John Kelly, we fired white phosphorus shells on their positions. Kelly had a vantage point that allowed him to accurately pinpoint the targets which he communicated back to us. Our first rounds were a direct hit. The phosphorus created a heavy white mist that illuminated the entire area. The minute Kelly saw that we were right on the target, he ordered us to follow up with volleys of HE heavy rounds, completely destroying the 88s and the Germans who fled the holes. The phosphorous was burning their skin, working itself deeper and deeper into their flesh. The few rounds we fired roused those Jerries out of their holes, and we alleviated a dangerous situation by putting them all out of their misery.

The fighting went on for days. We had the advantage of being dug in, but the Germans could have easily overrun us by their sheer numbers. We were probably outnumbered ten to one, but our small battalion held Malmady. By sheer determination, and a lot of luck, we held those Germans back. Till it was said and done, they got close enough to kill with hand grenades, but never got past us. Hitler's desperate push early in the Bulge cost him thousands of lives.

Just days before we arrived at Malmady, the Germans had captured about one hundred fifty American prisoners. I believe most of them were from the 285th Field Artillery, but there were also doctors and men from other outfits among them. They were paraded into a snow-covered field and machine gunned down. Freshly fallen snow covered their bodies. Miraculously there were a few dozen survivors. Although wounded and covered with snow, they lay quietly through the night, feigning death. Our battalion encountered a few of the survivors when we arrived in Malmady; a few medics were treating their wounds. It was this massacre at Malmady that prompted our new orders. We were told from this day forward, "Do not take prisoners."

Otto Skorzeny, one of Hitler's favorite SS commandos, implemented and commanded a plan conceived by Hitler, called Operation Greif, to infiltrate and cause confusion during the Ardennes offensive. Skorzeny had gained Hitler's respect when he flew into Italy by glider and rescued Mussolini from the clutches of the Allies. Operation Greif was simple and effective in that it succeeded in causing the Allies a great deal of confusion. Skorzeny sent English-speaking Germans, dressed in American uniforms, into the area, many as paratroopers, and others in American vehicles. They wreaked havoc by messing up communications, altering or removing road signs, and misdirecting traffic.

These activities created turmoil, sometimes allowing German soldiers to pass while American soldiers were detained. Our unit, being mostly Norwegian nationals and Norwegian Americans, suffered the occasional detainment of men due to their accents. They were thought to be German, especially when they were overhead speaking Norwegian. They were warned for their own safety to avoid speaking their native tongue.

Passwords were an absolute necessity to weed out infiltrators and were changed daily. For example, if someone shouted 'eagle,' you had damned well better answer 'nest.' Passwords changed every day and spread like wildfire among the men. Questions about American baseball teams, things that only Americans would know, were common. Unfortunately, some Americans who were not baseball fans found themselves detained because they could not answer questions about America's favorite pastime.

It was during this time when infiltrators were a problem that we took turns going out on patrols for a few hours at a time. I was sent out with a few guys with instructions to shoot down German paratroopers. Unfortunately for the Allies, most of Skorzeny's infiltrators were already on the ground, but it saved me the trouble of having to shoot men out of the sky, like hunting ducks on a fall day. Patrolling was usually a nighttime activity, but this particular mission was carried out in daylight, usually at dawn.

Zero visibility, the result of heavy snowfall for more than a week, prevented the Allies from taking to the skies. However, a couple of days before Christmas the snow finally let up, the skies cleared, and thousands of missions were flown over the next few days, driving the Germans back. On Christmas Day and the next two days, the American Air Force bombed Malmady. It was we, the 99th, who occupied Malmady, not the Germans as the Air Force mistakenly thought. It was a mess for us because we had to help evacuate the citizens while scrambling to save our own lives. There was a lot of confusion and a lot of destruction, and we couldn't understand the lack of communication with air support.

Despite all the noise from artillery and bombing, and the death and devastation that surrounded us, our battalion Chaplain, Paul Wharton, rounded up a small group and conducted a brief service in the hayloft of a barn on Christmas Day. Being together in that barn is one Christmas I will never forget. The day was bitterly cold, but I felt warm and comforted for the brief time we sat huddled together. Looking around at the men, I imagined that this is what having a family must feel like. I could feel the closeness, the security, the warmth and the joy.

Christmas had held little meaning to me before this day because of my lack of family stability; but in the eyes of the men assembled here, I saw its very special meaning. More than a celebration of the birth of Christ, it was a celebration of family as well. I'd listened to countless stories over campfires and Canned Heat as the men regaled each other with stories of home, tales of loving mothers and fathers waiting for the war to be over, for their beloved sons to come home. I had no first hand experience at being part of a real family, but I knew now that I wanted one of my own someday. The gentle sound of the Chaplain's voice brought me back to the present. I don't remember his words, but I am certain he prayed for our survival through the remaining days of the Bulge.

28
The New Year

By year's end the weather took a turn for the worse, and in spite of near zero visibility, the Luftwaffe took control of the sky on New Year's Day. In one last desperate but futile attempt, young German pilots climbed into their planes and took to the skies, diving, strafing, and bombing American aircraft grounded by the weather.

Our ground gunners had a field day shooting them out of the sky. Poor visibility caused many of them to crash, and others ran out of fuel and fell from the sky, exploding on impact. Some crashed just attempting to land. I remember shooting at the planes with a rifle as they flew low over the trees, just a couple of hundred feet off the ground. It was a lot like shooting at ducks, and almost as difficult. Even though the planes were a lot larger, they were a hell of a lot faster than a duck. Strangely, I found it entertaining to watch them dive toward the ground and burst into flames. It was quite a show. This was not the first time I observed planes crashing; I had seen American planes come down earlier in the war.

Well over a hundred grounded American planes were lost that first day of 1945, but the raid proved most devastating to the German air force. Over two hundred enemy planes were shot down or crashed, and three hundred enemy pilots lost their lives on that bitter cold day in Belgium.

On the 6th of January our battalion moved to an area near Stavelot, not far from Malmady, and dug ourselves in. We took turns going out on raids and patrols. By now, we were becoming exhausted. It was bitterly cold here at the Bulge, especially at night, so we took turns crawling from our foxhole into a basement that was very close by. Here we could be out of the wind and snow and get a little sleep. Most of the men, however, lived and slept outside, round the clock, mostly in foxholes or trenches, unprotected from the weather. There were very few places to take cover.

Frostbite was common and affected a lot of the men; I was lucky and didn't suffer greatly from it, even though I had no gloves. Later in life, however, I would experience the loss of sensation in some of my fingers and toes. I honestly don't know how in hell we survived that winter in the Ardennes.

Near the end of the Breakthrough, I was approached one day by a woman and her two young daughters. Her husband had been taken prisoner when the German army had occupied her small village just a few weeks before. Even though the Germans had been pushed out of the area, she, like many others, was terrified that 'Le Bosh,' as she called them, might be coming back. She pleaded with me to stop them as though I alone could perform a miracle. Even though I knew the Germans were just a few kilometers outside of town, dangerously close to us, I assured her that we would stop them, and that she should not be afraid. Her gratitude was profuse and her relief immeasurable as she smiled through her tears and returned to her home. Watching her depart, I prayed that we wouldn't let her down.

A few days later toward evening the same woman stopped by to see me. I was on a break, smoking a cigarette, as she asked in very broken English if I would come along with her. I followed her down the street and into a tiny church where a few dozen people had assembled for a service. Her two young daughters, wrapped in tattered woolen coats, were waiting for her there, sitting in a pew near the back of the sanctuary. She sat down next to her girls and whispered for me to take the seat beside her.

The service, though brief, kept me indoors just long enough to thaw my frozen limbs. I had been cold for too long. When the service ended, she took me to her modest home and shared what little food she had. Her kind gesture was her way of thanking me for keeping the Germans out of her town. I thanked her and walked the short distance back to my unit, overwhelmed by her effort to provide me some comfort. The food warmed my body and the service warmed my soul, and I never forgot the kindness shown me by a woman who had suffered so much and whose name I would never know.

29
Master Sergeant, Jack McCloskey

One bitterly cold morning I was huddled beside a pill box, high up on a hill, scanning the horizon in the direction of Liege. This area, including Malmady and Spa, was known as 'buzz bomb alley' because of heavy concentrations of buzz bombs that fell in this area, causing horrific damage. I was on guard duty this morning when I spotted antennas towering above the tree line about a half mile down the hill. I was certain the antennas belonged to 1st Army communications, my brother-in-law's outfit. My spirits rose at the prospect of seeing my sister's husband, and my good buddy, Jack. We hadn't seen each other for three years.

Quickly, I informed my buddies of my intention to investigate the antennas, and then sprinted down the hill and into the woods where I found several large communication trailers. Feeling hopeful, I called out Jack's name until men began pouring out of the trailers to see what all the excitement was about. Jack had come out as well, surprised to hear his name called, and stood there with the others. He looked me over carefully, a smile spreading across his ample face, and threw his arms around me in a bone-crushing embrace.

We hugged for a long moment until he took me inside to sit down and warm up, expressing concern over my haggard appearance. I quickly assured Jack that I was okay, but he was not convinced. He poured us each a cognac, and we celebrated our fortuitous meeting. I was quite impressed to learn that Jack was in charge of this particular trailer. He had done well for himself in the Army, and I was proud of him. Jack was like a brother to me, and I knew that though he was worried, he was proud of me, too.

We did some catching up and shared a few laughs before parting ways, making a promise to each other that we'd survive the war. Saying goodbye to Jack that chilly morning in Belgium was difficult for me. I banished from my thoughts a yearning for the little family I had, and sprinted uphill to my post on the mountain and the reality that I had been living for the past few years.

I learned many months later that Jack and the men of 1st Army Communications were nearly captured a few hours after my departure. They had gotten word that the Germans were coming, climbed into their trucks and got out with only minutes to spare.

The Battle of the Bulge ended for us on a cold January day. This was our last major battle with the Germans and had kept us on the front lines in the Malmady and Stavelot area for thirty-one non-stop days of fighting. By the 16th of January, 1945, the Allies had regained control of Belgium and had re-established their line. Thus began the push that would force the Germans back into Germany and ultimately bring the war to a close.

30
A Monastery in Belgium

One night in Belgium I was assigned guard duty in an ancient monastery that served as temporary quarters for an aid station. The monastery had sustained bomb damage, but remained mostly intact, offering some degree of protection for the wounded. Its ornate roof, built of large slate tiles, appeared to have suffered the most in that loose tiles hung precariously around holes and damaged areas. The massive building, located dangerously close to enemy territory, had many doors requiring more than a few guards. I was assigned to protect one area, a long, dark corridor, from any infiltrators attempting to enter. My orders—shoot to kill.

Reporting for duty early evening on the day of my assignment, I observed a small boy milling about alone by the main door. Children were rarely seen wandering around alone during the war; it was too dangerous. I don't know why he was there; he may have been orphaned and had no place to go. Only moments after I spotted him, a large tile slid from the damaged roof and struck him, splitting his head open. I had seen much bloodshed during my months in combat, but this visage made me sick to my stomach. I knew the boy was seriously injured and wasted no time rushing him inside.

Belgium had sustained a great deal of damage during the war, thus we were without electricity. No electricity for lights or other human conveniences; the war had seen to that. So, I was given a few small candles for light during the long night I stood watch. Burning only one candle at a time, I set a lighted candle carefully down on a small table, allowing a few drops of hot wax to secure it in place. The flame, flickering erratically in a draft, cast eerie shadows down the long stone corridor, ending in darkness as stark as the sadness I felt over the suffering of one small boy.

With the exception of my thoughts, I was completely alone the entire night, and in spite of my circumstances, felt no fear, only a strange sense of peace in my surroundings. The night was long, but uneventful. Sometime during the early morning hours, my attention was drawn to an old wooden box resting on the floor half way down the corridor. The box was about five feet long, a foot and a half wide, fragile and covered in dust. Giving in to my curiosity, I lifted the lid from the box and found the bones of a human being inside.

We had very few opportunities to amuse ourselves during the war, so I saw in this a chance for a little entertainment. Carefully, I took the bones from the box one at a time and put them into position on the floor, sort of like building a puzzle. I did this bone by bone until I had put the entire skeleton together, skull to toe. Much like a puzzle, some of the pieces were missing, and others were completely unfamiliar to me.

Just about the time I finished, my relief showed up, looking at me in disbelief. He was astonished at the sight of a human skeleton lying loosely on the floor and asked me, "What the hell are you doing?" We had a good laugh at my antics as we very carefully put the bones, piece by piece, back into the box.

Guard duty finished, I returned to my unit without learning the condition of the boy. Ignoring his fate left me with at least a shred of hope. Thinking back on the incident, however, I am quite certain the boy died from his wound, but I lacked the courage to hear those words at the time. I had already seen enough death and suffering to last a lifetime.

31
474th Infantry Regiment (Separate), Barneville, France

Exhausted after the Bulge, the battalion finally left the Malmady–Stavelot area around the 18th of January. We returned to Tilff, Belgium, for a brief rest before packing up for our move to Barneville, France. We were fed well, given a few days to rest and clean up, and were greatly relieved to finally change our clothes, the same clothing we had been living in for more than a month.

Rested up and ready to travel, we boarded a train in Tilff for our journey to Barneville. Although the train was crowded and the trip uncomfortable by ordinary human standards, resting on the floor evoked fond memories of my days on the lam, hopping freight trains, inhaling deeply my hand-rolled cigarettes, and exploring the world, bound to no one. As a boy, I feared only the police; they were the enemy then.

But this was now, and I was caught up in a completely different and frightening reality that I would put out of my mind for the next couple of days. Familiar voices, the rhythmic clanging sounds of the train, and the vibrations beneath the floor lulled me quickly into a deep and peaceful sleep. My solitude, disrupted momentarily during the night, quickly returned as I reminded myself that I wasn't in a foxhole anymore.

Three days on a train gave us ample time to think. We knew the war was not over, yet had no idea why we were headed for Barneville. We all felt a sense of dread of what was to come, and speculated that we might be headed for an invasion of Norway. Although our battalion had lost a lot of men, many of those who remained were Norwegians who were holding onto the hope of going to Norway. A few others just wanted to go home. Tired and weary for so long, they had seen enough war.

Having been with the 99th since Cherbourg, I had become very much one of them and desired to go wherever they went. In spite of the fact that I'd seen enough combat, and had no family connections whatsoever to Norway, I wanted to invade Norway as desperately as they, freeing the land they loved. Even though I had a hometown of my own, I really had no home to go back to. The Army had become my home now, the only stability I had ever known, and in these Norwegian men, I had found a family.

Barneville was no longer the beautiful and prosperous town of pre-war days. Much of it now lay in rubble, almost completely destroyed. Its citizens, though free now, were poor and struggling to survive, and many of them were homeless.

Our battalion set up camp in a deserted resort by the sea. The place was not fancy, but offered a beautiful view of the English Channel, and hot food was a daily event. The recently formed 474th Infantry Regiment (Separate) was stationed here. We soon learned that we were brought here to become part of the 474th and would be training with them to prepare for the invasion of Norway. The 474th was formed from what was left of the First Special Service Force (a Canadian American

Regiment), a few Rangers, and some officers and enlisted men from the 552nd Anti-Tank Company.

Much like the 99th Infantry Battalion (Separate), the First Special Service Force was an elite outfit organized in mid-1942 for the purpose of covert operations in occupied Norway. That mission was scratched and the FSSF headed to Italy where it began its distinct reputation of overcoming impossible odds. It, too, began as volunteers, forest rangers, lumber jacks and others, who became highly trained commandos in mountain fighting, amphibious warfare, explosives, stealth and hand-to-hand combat. The FSSF saw a lot of action in Italy and Southern France and suffered the loss of many fine men. While in Anzio, Italy, the FSSF earned the name 'Devil's Brigade,' where, in a diary taken from a dead German soldier, was written, "The black devils are all around us..." The men of the FSSF were notorious for painting their faces black for nighttime raids and were absolutely feared by the Germans.

Our new insignia, consisting of the 99[th's] Viking ship, the FSSF's red arrowhead, and a bar representing the Rangers, became a symbol of great pride for all of us. Merged now, and about 3,000 men strong, we became the 474th Infantry Regiment (Separate) under the command of Colonel Edwin Walker. My company, Company D, a heavy weapons company, from this day forward would be called Company M of the 99th Infantry Battalion (Separate), under the 474th Inf. Regiment (Separate). Although we were merged together as a single regiment, we would be split up many times in the weeks ahead. The 'Separate' designation we carried as a battalion and now as a regiment meant simply that we were not a part of any larger unit. We were used for special missions, usually involving a great deal of danger, often splitting up, then coming back together again after the mission was carried out. We were a proud unit; I know that I speak for every man in the battalion when I say that it was an honor to serve with the 99th Infantry Battalion (Separate).

As history soon proved, the Germans in occupied Norway surrendered and agreed to Allied conditions regarding their peaceful evacuation and the removal of prisoners and misplaced persons. It was mutually agreed that their evacuation would take place with the help of the newly formed 474th Infantry Regiment (Separate). However, it is interesting to note that, in the event the Germans had not willingly agreed to surrender in this way, but instead had chosen to retreat under their own organization and supervision, the decision was made to send the 99th Infantry Battalion (Separate) into Norway to serve as bodyguards for the returning king, while the Germans evacuated themselves.

During our mostly peaceful stay in Barneville, more than a thousand Germans who had been holed up the Channel Islands throughout the war raided the French coastline in an unexpected attack. They had run out of supplies and were desperate for food, fuel, and anything else they could get their hands on. The islands had been deliberately bypassed by the Allies during the D-Day invasion for fear of harming civilians living there. I remember seeing lights going out on the islands as they ran out of fuel to run their generators. Without fuel, they were left without electricity for light and communications.

When the raids ceased, we patrolled the coast round the clock, keeping an eye out for any further trouble. Caution was the order of the day, not because of German snipers, but because of land mines hidden all over the beaches, and inland as well. This act of German ingenuity kept our engineers busy detonating and removing land mines for weeks to come.

The 474th's daily training included lectures and familiarization with new weapons and equipment. We had an armored section now, tanks and M-8 armored cars, and became familiar with their operation and use as well. The only problems we encountered during training involved mortar shells falling short of their targets, injuring some of the men in the field. The filaments were defective, causing the mortars to misfire and fall short. Other than these few mishaps with the mortars, training went smoothly until the end of March when we were finally given our new orders. We would follow Patton's Third Army into Germany, rounding up SS troops, cleaning up pockets of Germans hiding, missed, or left behind, and freeing people imprisoned by the Germans. In the weeks ahead we would be grateful for our intensive training, as this new mission would prove to be dangerous business.

32
Paris

On the 2nd of April, the 474th shipped out by truck and headed for Aachen, Germany. The roads were in deplorable shape and slowed us down considerably, and land mines were still a potential threat. Our convoy made a few brief stops en route for meals and pit stops, but mostly we kept moving. We stopped every few hours for a 'piss call,' whereupon we'd leap off the trucks, line up shoulder to shoulder along the side of the road, and relieve ourselves. The French people found this behavior very strange; we found their reactions amusing. However, when setting up camp for the night, we'd dig a small trench to serve as our latrine, and then cover it up carefully the next morning before moving out.

Along the way we passed through many towns and villages that were nothing more than piles of rubble. There was just so much destruction from the war. Villages that had stood for centuries were suddenly gone. Europe would never be the same.

Paris, liberated in August of last year, provided a memorable stopover for the regiment. People in the streets immediately came over to our convoy and handed us flowers and bottles of wine and cognac. Leaping from our trucks, we gratefully accepted their hospitality. The reception, though unexpected, was joyful as many of the citizens hugged us, repeating over and over, "Merci, American, merci." I felt overwhelmed by their gratitude and proud that I had played a small part in liberating so many people.

We pulled crackers and treats from our kits and dug into our pockets for chocolate bars for the children who had assembled around us. Many of them, with reaching arms, wanted to be picked up and held by an American soldier. It was an honor to hold the children and watch them smile. Reveling in the joy on the faces of these Parisians, I understood what our sacrifice was for.

The convoy made a brief pit stop near a large cemetery. A few of the guys and I trotted over to investigate. Walking through the cemetery, we realized this was the final resting place for hundreds of Americans who died in World War I. There were British, French, and others as well. I felt like I had stepped back in time as I gazed at all the different markers in memory of so many brave young men. Saddened that so many Americans were left behind, it suddenly occurred to me that my buddies and I were being left behind as well. Our convoy had started without us and we had to run like hell to catch up.

Paris had sustained some damage, but we didn't see much of it as we traveled quickly through town. I remember seeing the Eiffel Tower for the first time in my life, gazing at it with stoic indifference. I could summon no interest or curiosity whatsoever. Perhaps in another time, when the world had come to its senses, I would be able to look at things differently again, but not now. I had to stay focused on the weeks ahead.

I left Paris lost in a state of reverie, filled with smiling faces and fortified with hope. However, the dramatically changing vista snapped me back to reality when I realized we had departed Paris and everything around us lay in ruins.

33
Cleaning Up After Patton

The journey to Aachen was uneventful as far as encounters with the enemy were concerned, but memorable otherwise. All across France we witnessed the sacrifices made by civilians struggling to survive in their bombed cities, salvaging what they could of their homes and belongings. We also saw huge POW camps that housed thousands of German prisoners inside large barbed wire enclosures, who, ironically, were better fed than the ordinary citizens in France.

A few days later the 474th arrived in Aachen. Like many other towns in Europe, Aachen was severely damaged; many structures were completely gone. I remember thinking what a mess it was; people were hiding in their cellars because they were so afraid of us. They had been told that Americans would kill them. This, of course, was untrue.

We quickly settled in for our short stay, bedding down anywhere we could find shelter. The Regiment split up and spread out far and wide, searching houses and buildings, and patrolling Aachen and its vast surroundings in search of any leftover enemy soldiers. Rounding up SS troops was high on our list. Many had retreated into Germany and were hiding. They were not stupid and knew they would be executed even if they surrendered. German soldiers dressed in civilian clothes were rounded up as well.

SS troops were Hitler's elite killing machines. Refusing to be captured, many perished. Capturing them was dangerous business; they were haughty and resourceful. Interrogating them was futile; they cursed us but divulged no secrets. I'll never forget one I captured near the end of the war, the most arrogant of all. He had red hair like me. He was cold and calculating right to the end, showing absolutely no trace of fear.

Although civilians resented our thorough searches of their homes, they offered no resistance. Some even assisted us in pinpointing the whereabouts of SS troops or Nazis and other individuals considered criminals of war. The Germans were a sad people, a defeated people, and I felt deeply sorry for them.

All through the war, I never thought of Germans as evil. They were human beings, a bit misguided, young men like me, sons and brothers, who didn't want to be here any more than I did. But it was drilled into my head that the Germans were the enemy, and I knew it was essential for my own survival and the success of the campaign that I not forget it. Therefore, I had no choice but to adopt a kill-or-be-killed attitude. Kill without thought, without regret; that was my duty. There would be plenty of time for remorse later.

Going even deeper into Germany, I headed south with my unit. In a heavily wooded area a few miles outside of Aachen, we encountered snipers and dealt swiftly with them. Those who refused to surrender died. At this point, most Germans were exhausted and tired of the war. Knowing defeat was imminent, they began surrendering to us by the hundreds. Over the next couple of weeks, the 474th had its hands full processing prisoners and displaced persons, and accumulating enemy weapons and ammunition along the way.

After leaving Aachen, the 99th crossed the Rhine River searching the woods and villages for days. Once we were certain that the enemy was gone, we headed to Heroldsbach where we patrolled and checked things out there as well. We took a lot of prisoners during our brief stay.

In Heroldsbach my Company took up residence in a castle, surrounded on three sides by water, situated just on the edge of town. The structure served as our temporary base camp and was quite luxurious compared to sleeping on the ground, even though we slept on the floor. It had an enormous facade and high ceilings throughout, and a bridge over a moat. Fortunately it had sustained only minor damage from the war and was still very beautiful. It appeared to be devoid of human inhabitants; perhaps they had taken up residence in the basement, as was common all through Europe. We spent several days in Heroldsbach, residing in a castle, until our work was finished.

34
A Close Call

We were rapidly approaching the end of the war and, by some miracle, I had survived. However, I was nearly killed one afternoon during a close encounter with a very inebriated American soldier. It happened while we were rounding up prisoners, searching houses, and patrolling in Germany.

I overheard a commotion coming from a house very nearby and went over to see what was going on. A man was cursing loudly and making threats. An American soldier, belonging to a trucking outfit passing through town, was threatening an elderly German couple, demanding they give him liquor. He held them at gunpoint just outside the front of their home and angrily waved his loaded pistol in the air. The man and woman were terrified.

His behavior was inexcusable; the men in my battalion never mistreated or threatened civilians. Although we were always cautious, civilians were handled with a great deal of respect, often giving aid to them when possible. Because the soldier was drunk, I knew he would probably kill the couple, and I was not going to let that happen. So I said to him, "Hey, soldier, let these people alone. Follow me and I'll show you where you can get something to drink."

After a long, tense couple of minutes, I convinced him to give me the pistol, a German P38 'souvenir' he had picked up somewhere. Surprised that he handed over the pistol, I continued talking calmly to him while removing and emptying the clip, and extracting a bullet from the chamber. Slowly I handed the gun back to him and said, "Come on, let's go," and he followed me. My intention was to take him back to his outfit.

Although we left the house together, I walked a few strides in front of him. We'd gone only a short distance when I heard the slide of his pistol and knew the man had reloaded. I turned slowly and faced him. He looked directly at me and said, "You are not going nowhere." He'd obviously changed his mind and was pointing the pistol, at very close range, directly at me. Realizing my error, I muttered a profanity and calmly said, "Put the gun away and let's go." Glaring, he cursed me and pulled the trigger.

Armed with a .45 caliber pistol, I could easily have killed him, but I didn't want to face the consequences. Instead, I spun on my heels and sprinted toward a rise in the road just ahead of me, while ducking and dodging bullets. When I reached the rise, I leapt over the railroad tracks along the top and dove down the other side. He fired at me several times until his pistol was empty.

I was about a tenth of a mile ahead of him when a soldier armed with a rifle came running towards me. He asked what all the shooting was about and I told him. "One of your guys is shooting at me," I said. He replied, "Let's go get him!" I looked at him coolly and said, "If you want him, you go get him," and I went back to work.

35
Buchenwald

Our mission took us deeper and deeper into Germany as we cleaned out more towns and woodlands. Our journey from Heroldsbach took us into Bavaria for more of the same. This mission also gave us our first glimpse of concentration camps. On our way to Nuremberg we stopped just north of Buchenwald, located in central Germany. I was part of a large group of men chosen to go into the camp. I had no idea that what I was about to witness would change my life forever.

Buchenwald was a Class II concentration camp, one of the largest in Germany, built on top of a hill surrounded by fields. Its sole purpose was the incarceration of political prisoners for use as slave laborers, many of whom were Communists. These prisoners from dozens of ethnic backgrounds, including Germans, were considered dangerous, a high level threat to Germany. They were not brought here for execution, but many would die as a result. There were doctors, college professors, and politicians among the 60,000 or so people who were estimated to have been imprisoned here. Buchenwald was not a death camp. Jews were not brought here to be gassed. In fact, very few Jews were brought to Buchenwald initially; and those who came were kept separately from the general population. Later, towards the end of the war as some of the other camps shut down, Jews were marched to Buchenwald, but very few survived the journey.

We arrived in Buchenwald a day or two after it was liberated. Prisoners were milling about in various states of dress and undress. Their clothing was filthy and torn. Some wore nothing at all. Many were dazed, others staggered, some crawled, and many couldn't even rise to their feet. The living were more gruesome than the dead. It is hard to imagine a human being so frail, so corpse-like, yet still alive and breathing. At least the dead no longer suffered.

Inside the barracks, men were packed four or five to a bunk, skeletons covered with flesh, many barely alive, with big glary eyes. There were rows and rows of them. Some were standing, but many could not get up; they were too weak. There were Hungarians, Poles, Yugoslavs, Russians, Czechs, Germans, and many others. We were told not to feed them for fear of making them sick.

I spoke to them, but they didn't understand me, as most of them spoke no English. I shook their hands and patted their backs, feeling strangely drawn to them; their smiles portraying a depth of joy heretofore unknown to me. They were free now, and they knew it. The compassion I felt for those men broke my heart that day. They were smiling and happy even though many of them probably wouldn't survive the day. At least they would die free men. This was the most pathetic thing I had ever seen in my life. And the smell... I had smelled death every day for months, but this was different. I will never forget it.

Outside the buildings lay piles of human bodies in the most revolting shades of gray, stacked like cords of wood. In death, each one had been stripped of his clothing before being summarily stacked in alternating rows.

Many German citizens were not aware of the atrocities that had taken place here; or more likely, they simply chose to deny it. By order of General Patton, we marched the townspeople from neighboring towns through the camp. They needed to see what was going on in their own backyards. We did as we were told, rounding them up and parading them through, men, women and children. No one was exempt. They were horrified; many of them covered their eyes. Many wept.

By war's end, only 20,000 prisoners in Buchenwald were still alive, all of them slaves, many near death. All through the war, hundreds of them died each day. They were forced to work long hours, day after day, in nearby factories while subsisting on one meal a day—a slice of bread and a bowl of stew. Most of them died from disease, exhaustion, and starvation, but others were beaten or executed.

There were no gas chambers here, just a crematorium to dispose of bodies. However, the Germans had run short on fuel for the ovens and could not keep up with the one hundred human beings who died each day. So they dug a ditch and tossed in each day's quota; in life stripped of dignity, in death stripped naked. There were hundreds, perhaps thousands, already stacked one atop the other, their proximity suffocating, yet strangely comforting in that, in death, they were not alone.

Anger welled up from deep inside me, anger for the Nazis, the perpetrators of this heinous act against fellow human beings, and anger for what I would become in the weeks ahead for having borne witness at Buchenwald. I resolved to kill those responsible for these atrocities, and there would be opportunities before the war was over.

36
Nuremberg

As was often the case, my battalion split up around the time that I was in Buchenwald. By signed order of General Patton, some of the men in my outfit were assigned a top secret mission guarding a large convoy of vehicles traveling from Merkers to Frankfort, Germany. The convoy carried works of art, gold bullion and currency valued at more than two billion dollars; treasures that had been confiscated by the Nazis and stored in salt mines in Merkers. Also recovered in the mines were sacks of gold fillings taken from the mouths of holocaust victims. The convoy tied up the Autobahn for eighty miles, permitting no one to pass, as P-47s and small aircraft took to the air for additional support. The convoy arrived safely in Frankfort and the treasures were placed in a bank vault for safekeeping.

After Buchenwald, we regrouped and headed for Nuremberg to round up SS troops, Nazis, and war criminals. The town had been heavily bombed shortly before we arrived and many people were dead or dying. The town's people were in shock from the bombing and gave us little or no resistance. Many residents were hiding in basements and shelters because they feared the Americans; they were certain we would harm them.

We had an enormous responsibility here in Nuremberg; it was a sprawling town. We went from door to door, barging right in, kicking down doors that were locked. Conducting house to house searches to flush out SS troops was becoming routine; we'd done so much of it. However, we never let our guard down, not even for a second, as each house or barn or building to be searched held the potential for death—our death. A trapped Nazi was a dangerous foe.

Edgy after Buchenwald, and exhausted from lack of sleep, I kicked down a locked door when I heard shuffling sounds inside. Cast in shadows, the room was darker than I expected, but I noticed a subtle movement beneath a large round table. Hiding when ordered to surrender was a self-imposed death sentence, and certain that I'd found another Nazi, I sent the table flying with one powerful kick, exposing a middle-aged man in torn clothing. He was neither a Nazi, nor a soldier, but an unarmed man paralyzed with fear, certain I would kill him. And I nearly did. What stopped me from pulling the trigger was the look on his face. No human being should ever have to know that kind of fear. He had suffered enough, having survived the prior night's bombing, and he had no legs. His torso sat directly on the floor in a grotesque kind of way. Glancing quickly around the room, I finished my search and let the man be, although I will never forgot the look of horror on his face.

I remember searching a bombed out hotel and finding a woman in an upstairs room. Alone, she sat huddled over a bundle in her lap and did not acknowledge my presence. Her head hung low as she sat on a bed cradling a baby in her arms. The child was an eerie shade of blue; its body was bloated and its face was swollen. I could see that the baby was dead. It had probably died as a result of bombs that fell on Nuremberg during the night. I cannot imagine how long she must have sat there holding her dead child. Though wrought with grief, she looked slowly up at me, as though in a trance, and mumbled the words, "Hitler, no good." I should have been numb by now from all the death I'd witnessed, but the lump in my throat reminded me that I still could feel. Unable to form words to comfort the woman, to tell her everything would soon be alright, I nodded my response instead, went on with my work, and never looked back.

Finished in Nuremberg, the battalion moved out, encountering some resistance before arriving in Regenstauf. Many Germans, afraid of being captured or killed, shed their uniforms and dressed as civilians. We were not easily fooled, however, as their age and physical appearance gave them away. Germany was in dire need of men, especially during the last months of the war, so every male in Germany, with the exception of children, elderly or infirm, was needed to fight. Simply, we rounded up every healthy German male between the ages of 16 and 60.

Regenstauf harbored Germans who surrendered willingly and a few Nazis holed up in town who didn't. With very little resistance our work was finished quickly and the battalion moved on. Our final stop was Regensburg. Sometime before our arrival, we were given the wonderful news that just a few days earlier, on May 8, 1945, the war in Europe had ended. The news spread fast, and tired, weary German soldiers, hundreds of them, threw down their guns, and suddenly began surrendering to us in Regensburg, knowing they would be treated humanely.

Sorting through countless prisoners was an unexpected event that kept us busy for days. The surrender went smoothly, and I don't recall encountering any problems with prisoners. Germany had lost the war, and I truly believe these young men didn't care. They were exhausted and weary and had been hungry for too long. I actually felt sorry for them.

PART FOUR

37
Norway

Relieved that the war in Europe had finally ended, we loaded our gear and ourselves into trucks and left Regensburg by the middle of May and headed for Duclair, France. As our convoy crossed the border into Belgium, I watched the German countryside fade away into the distance and wished I could have left the memories behind as well. Our journey of more than 500 miles would take us through Belgium and across France for the fourth and final time. Told that we would be going to Norway lifted our spirits considerably. But first we were given a few days rest in Duclair.

Relaxed, cleaned up, and sporting new uniforms, equipment and vehicles, we left Duclair and traveled to LeHarve on the French coast. On the 29th of May the Regiment boarded LSTs and spent the first night in the harbor on board ship. The following morning our convoy of thirteen LSTs and one cargo ship headed into the English Channel toward the North Sea and then on to Norway.

There were only 3,000 of us, one regiment, going to Norway. Our mission was an extremely important one: disarm and repatriate 350,000 Germans, including high ranking officers. Not great odds. Told that they had surrendered and would lay down their arms, we were somewhat reassured, but had learned never to let our guard down. Though I was excited to be going to Norway, I felt the slightest twinge of trepidation.

Expecting little or no resistance, there were no guarantees that this would be a peaceful evacuation. In addition to disarming and repatriating all 350,000 German troops, we would be organizing displaced persons and prisoners (Russians and others) for shipment to their home countries. We would also be guarding and disabling strategic installations, like German 88s, brought to Norway by the Germans.

The journey to Norway was leisurely with lots of free time to socialize. We ate good food and enjoyed warm weather and calm seas. The men, through clearly relieved that our combat days were behind us, could only think about Norway. Many hadn't seen their families since before the occupation. For some of them Norway was home. They were Norwegian sailors who became stranded in the U.S. when Germany occupied Norway. Unable to return home, they were given U.S. citizenship, and then joined the 99th Infantry Battalion (Separate). For others Norway was their second home; many of their relatives lived in Norway. The men spoke endlessly of family, friends, and hometowns in Norway. I was delighted for them; their reverie and laughter brought me joy. I'd never seen the men happier than they were on this day.

The beautiful Norwegian language flowed from the mouths of the men in a melody as joyous as their mood. They no longer had to fear being mistaken for the enemy. All the men of the 99th, except for replacements like me, spoke fluent Norwegian. I had picked up words and phrases during my tour of Europe with them, but it was during this voyage and in the months ahead, that I would become more familiar with the language. I had learned many French words and phrases as well, but I preferred Norwegian. It had a nice ring to it, and the men enjoyed teaching me. Perhaps my fondness for the language had something to do with the fact that I had come to love the Norwegian people, first the guys in my battalion, then during my stay in Smestad. Norwegians are a caring, gracious and loving people, and I would never forget the hospitality shown me over the next few months.

Early into our journey, our comradery was disrupted by gunfire and followed by a loud explosion. Diligent sailors on board had spotted and detonated a mine in the water. Throughout the entire trip, they were on constant lookout for mines floating in the sea. The mines were quite large, round with a lot of fingers on them, and fairly easy to spot. We encountered quite a few, but they proved to be easy targets, and the men dispatched them effortlessly with just a few rounds from their rifles. The resulting explosions were huge and somewhat entertaining to watch. However, we had a great deal of respect for these weapons; hitting just one would have been disastrous.

After nearly a week at sea with balmy weather and sunshine, we arrived in Norway on a rainy day. I was awestruck by this ruggedly beautiful country that seemed to go up one hill and down the other. I soon learned that two-thirds of Norway is mountainous, and its beautiful rugged coastline is punctuated with inlets and thousands of islands. As we traveled into one of the inlets, the Oslo Fjord, I noticed the steep mountains on either side seemed to be closing in on us. Actually we were just nearing the end of the inlet, the port of Drammen, where we would be dropping off some men and vehicles. The rest of us sailed on to Oslo, and because our barracks in Smestad were not completely vacated, we spent the night on board and awaited transportation to Smestad in the morning. However, we were given passes for Oslo that evening, and took turns going into town. We were in Norway!

The sun rose slower than usual that first morning in Norway; perhaps it had higher summits to climb, or more likely, we had forgotten the meaning of patience. The men were very aware of the seriousness of their mission, but their hearts and minds were filled with Norway and loved ones. Finally, the order was given to go ashore, and our LSTs dropped their front ends, allowing men and vehicles to disembark. The men wasted no time filing out of the ships in an orderly fashion and into trucks for the drive to our camp in Smestad, just north of Oslo.

Settling in quickly, we got down to the serious business at hand. There was so much to be done, but our first important duty was preparing for the return of King Haakon VII. The king had been exiled in England for five long years and would be returning to his beloved Norway on June 7, 1945, to a joyous nation and a celebration unlike anything I would ever witness again.

38
Honor Guard for King Haakon VII

Shortly after arriving in Oslo, I was informed by my commanding officer that I was one of a handful of men chosen to be part of an Honor Guard for King Haakon VII. The Honor Guard was made up of a few British and Norwegian soldiers and a few men chosen from the 99th Infantry Battalion (Separate). This was truly an honor, and I felt very proud to have been chosen.

On the morning of June 7th, we readied ourselves in full dress uniform, wearing our patches, and patiently lined up, three men deep, by the dock, awaiting the king's arrival. Haakon and his family arrived on the British Cruiser HMS Norfolk escorted by five destroyers. The rest of the men from the 99th were assigned as security guards along the route to be followed by the king as he traveled to the palace. Some of the men were armed and instructed to patrol specific areas, while others manned tanks.

Later that morning, King Haakon VII finally stepped onto the dock in Oslo. We, his Honor Guard, stood proudly in place, encircling him on three sides, three men deep. I remember being right up front when he walked over, looked directly at us and saluted. His smile was humble and I thought he was going to cry. The gratitude he felt for the Allies and

Americans who had freed his country was profoundly visible in his eyes. I will never forget it.

Then he spoke to us and to the enormous crowd that had gathered to welcome him home. The tumultuous roar of the crowd was deafening as the people of Norway cheered their King. After finishing his speech he acknowledged his Honor Guard again before being transported by car to the Palace. This was an emotional day for him and the people of Norway, a great day of celebration.

Hundreds of American, British, and Norwegian soldiers lined the route. Tens of thousands of Norwegians from all over the nation lined the streets, singing, dancing, cheering, and hoping for a glimpse of their king. It was estimated that half the population of Norway turned out to welcome King Haakon home. The citizens stood for hours waiting patiently in the rain. This very emotional homecoming was probably the largest gathering of citizens that Oslo had ever seen. The Norwegian people finally had their freedom, and now they had their king. The celebrations lasted well into the night. This was certainly one of the most memorable days of my life.

39

Smestad

Three hundred and fifty thousand German soldiers and officers remaining in Norway were good to their word. Though defeated, they were proud people who conducted themselves in a peaceful and cooperative manner, handing over their weapons without a hitch, making easier the monumental task before us. Like us, they just wanted the war to be over; they wanted to go home to Germany, to their lives and their families.

We, the 474th Infantry Regiment (Separate), were a highly experienced, trained, and productive outfit, setting about each assignment with ardent ambition. In the months ahead, we would make swift work of organizing, containing, and repatriating the Germans, and found it a privilege to free and send home the many Russians and other displaced souls who had been enslaved during the war.

Much of our time was spent guarding prisoners, warehouses, and anti-aircraft installations (German 88's), located in the higher elevations. Quite a few weapons had been installed in the mountains of Norway, and most were still intact for firing. The guns were eventually disabled, but we took turns traveling up mountain roads, making rounds to prevent unauthorized individuals from tampering with any of these installations.

I often wondered how we got all those prisoners out of Smestad; there were so many of them. The German prisoners were sorted by our officers, and then large groups were assigned to us. We'd pick them up at their compound, load them into trucks, and deliver them to the railroad station a few miles away. There the prisoners boarded boxcars for shipment to the coast. We were armed, of course, but no one ever gave us any trouble. We treated the Germans with respect and dignity during the entire evacuation process. They were respectful to us, as well, speaking quietly among themselves. They were exhausted and happy, relieved that they were going home. I remember that many of them actually smiled at us.

High ranking German officers were held in a Gestapo camp, enclosed with barbed wire, and kept separate from the regular prisoners who were hardly contained at all. Though they were not free to come and go as they pleased, the regular prisoners were housed in a variety of buildings around Smestad with minimum security. I recall seeing the German officers lining up for roll call, but I did not have any dealings with them personally. One could tell they had a great deal of pride, a lot of 'attitude,' and found it difficult to be lined up, disarmed, and generally treated like the prisoners they were. They, like all our prisoners, were treated humanely, though they may have been considered war criminals and dealt with as such. Fortunately, the whole evacuation process went smoothly and quickly.

Things were going very well for us in Smestad, and we found ourselves on the receiving end of a lot of free passes into town. The Norwegian people were grateful to us for removing thousands of German soldiers from their country, and hundreds of invitations arrived at Smestad inviting the men to visit, dine, and socialize with the locals. As luck would have it, we were urged to accept the invitations, but strongly advised to be on our very best behavior. Thus, our free time in Norway became a vacation of sorts, and the conduct of the men of the 99th proved exemplary.

Dining with the locals was a wonderful educational and cultural experience. I personally accepted many invitations and met many Norwegian families. Everyone fed us; we ate lots of delicious Norwegian food. It was here in Norway where I learned to appreciate fish, mostly salmon and kippered herring, gourmet treats to this very day. Some of my Norwegian buddies in the 99th took me along with them to visit with family and relatives. Often the family members served as tour guides, showing us the sights around Oslo. This is how I met two young ladies, sisters Yeanni and Bjorg, daughters of a couple whose invitation to dinner I had accepted. I became fond of Yeanni and Bjorg and their family, and I spent many hours with them, visiting the sights in Oslo and horseback riding in camp.

Together we visited a museum in town that housed ancient Viking ships. I held a personal fascination for Vikings and their dragon-headed longships, and became enthralled at the sight of these sleek vessels, imagining what it must have been like to have been a Viking more than a millennium ago. I thought about fearless Viking warriors sailing turbulent seas, raiding and striking terror in medieval Europe as powerful and dominant assailants. Then I returned to the present and remembered. How ironic that my own Viking Battalion had recently struck terror in the hearts of Europeans (Germans), setting out on raids, powerful and dominant assailants subduing a different kind of foe.

A good deal of my time was spent horseback riding around camp. We had a barn full of beautiful horses; half a dozen or so that we were permitted to ride at our whim. Although I am not certain, I believe those fine Norwegian horses were used by German Officers who were stationed here in Smestad during the German occupation of Norway

Because I loved horses, I went frequently to the barn, tossed a saddle on the back of my favorite mount, and went for a ride. The military saddles available for our use were not very comfortable, and I recall being unable to neck rein those horses. This wasn't the Wild West, after all. I was in Europe, the land of civilized riding, where people rode in the style of the English: one rein in each hand, directing one's mount with subtle hands and legs. Right rein, right turn; left rein, left turn, and so on. Being a rather bright fellow, I adapted readily and found the greatest pleasure taking in the beautiful Norwegian countryside from the back of such a splendid steed.

Often Yeanni, Bjorg, and a few of the men joined me on a ride, and we'd spend hours on horseback taking in the sights around us. I rode out alone only occasionally, and often to the rhythm of clattering pots and pans, provided by my fellow 99ers in a futile attempt to frighten my mount. The brave fellow, whom I had come to trust, would oblige with a few fancy steps, careful not to toss me off. The guys got a big kick out of watching the horse dance, but he eventually became bored of their antics and soon learned to move past them with little more than a snort.

Clubs, scattered around town and camp, were good places to get a bite to eat, socialize, or just hang out. There was always music and often dancing, great places to take the girls. I remember playing guitar and singing with one of my Norwegian buddies in Smestad. I played an acoustic guitar, and he played a steel guitar. We'd sing our hearts out, entertaining anyone drunk enough to listen. We sang country music, heartbreakers like *No Letter Today* and *Old Shep;* the latter being a real tearjerker. However, after a couple of drinks, we usually forgot the words; after a few more drinks we forgot the chords as well. Those were good times.

The Fourth of July was a special day for American soldiers in Norway. We celebrated our own independence with a parade down the main street of Oslo, as American planes roared overhead. Once again, Norwegian citizens assembled in the streets, this time celebrating an American holiday. Our military put on quite an impressive display, making this day a proud one for Americans in Norway.

By early August, we had made a great deal of progress in the sorting and distribution of prisoners. However, we were still busy guarding warehouses filled with goods confiscated by the Germans.

Guard duty was never any fun, except when I was assigned to guard a warehouse filled with the best quality wines, liquors, cognacs, and champagnes, all stolen from the French by the Germans during the war. When finished with my shift for the day, I'd take along a couple of bottles and sometimes a whole case of whatever I wanted, usually my favorite, Benedictine. Guarding this warehouse was a popular assignment, and there were many volunteers for the job. Each, like me, was rewarded by helping himself to a bottle or two, or maybe a case, and no one ever questioned us. After all, there was plenty to go around.

In early September, the battalion received the wonderful news that the Japanese had surrendered. The war in the Pacific was finally over. The world had returned to its senses and I was ecstatic, overjoyed. I wanted to cry; instead I got drunk and celebrated with the men. We all celebrated.

The world was finally at peace. No more killing, no more hunger, no more living in fear. Many years would pass before Europe would be rebuilt, and many years before its people would learn to live at ease with a neighbor who had brought so much death and terror to the world. But it would come, in time.

We found one final reason for celebration before shipping out—Norway's independence—and pulled it off with one last parade with all the pomp and circumstance it deserved. Our work here in Norway was finished, and we had to face the sad realization that most of us would soon leave her behind. But not the memories. I would never let them go. The months in Norway had strengthened me, and I hoped the memories I'd made would sustain me for a long time to come.

For one last time Norway's citizens came out in great numbers. Our presence in Norway had given them a sense of security, and now they lined the docks in Oslo Harbor in a show of gratitude. Rows upon rows of people waved good bye in the most bittersweet farewell as we boarded the SS Bienville for our final voyage home to America.

* * * * *

Author's Note: In the sixty years since the war ended, my father never had another sip of Benedictine even though he would occasionally remember it. So, one morning when we were about half way finished writing our book, I decided to stop at the liquor store and look it up. There on the top shelf in the liqueur section sat two bottles. I promptly purchased one and took it home. As usual, my father and I had gotten together that morning to work on our book. I grabbed two glasses from the cupboard, pulled the bottle from the bag, opened it, and handed it to my father. With a twinkle in his eye and a smile on his face, he put the bottle to his lips and savored that lovely long-awaited elixir from the past.

40
Going Home

I was reluctant to leave; my time in Norway had been a great experience, a vacation compared to the war, and saying goodbye was difficult. It was hard for the men to leave relatives behind. Some were given their discharges and were permitted to remain with their families in Norway, but most of the men went home to the States to be discharged. Some had married Norwegian women and had to leave them behind for the time being. Those who'd joined the battalion later in the campaign in Europe were young replacements who still had some service time left. They were sent to Germany to serve out their time with the occupation forces. I had more points than I needed before I went to Norway.

On the 16th of October, 1945, the 99th Infantry Battalion (Separate) sailed from Oslo Harbor on the converted freighter, Bienville, for Southampton, England. We dropped off some British soldiers, spent the night, and then sailed out to sea for Boston the next morning. One day out of Southampton, we encountered a severe storm. Already too far out to turn back, we steamed forward, riding out the storm as best as possible. Fortunately, the storm was short lived, but the waves were rough for days, making some of the guys sick. We encountered more mines, which kept the sailors on board busy.

Passing by our port side was the huge aircraft carrier, Enterprise. She was a very fast ship and left us quickly in her wake. On board were thousands of American servicemen who were being transported home to the States. The Enterprise had seen a lot of battles in the Pacific and had sustained damage several times. During one attack her forward elevator had been blown hundreds of feet into the air by a bomb-laden kamikaze plane. The waves rose so high that at times we could not see the Enterprise.

With the exception of the storm which left some of the men sick, our voyage to the States was restful. I spent many hours on deck with my buddies. They talked non-stop about their homes and families and their plans for the future; I mostly listened, not wanting to think about what was next for me.

Being an early riser, I typically spent an hour or so alone on deck before being joined by the guys. Heading towards the bow, my favorite place to reflect, the thought occurred to me that I was always looking ahead, to the future I guess, never behind at that which had passed. Thinking that I was alone this morning, I pulled a letter from my pocket and unfolded its fragile pages. I had carried this letter for quite some time as this was one of the few letters I received during the war; my sister wasn't much of a writer. Ironically, the letter was from Rosemary, the same Rosemary whose picture I cast into the sea four years earlier. I had forgotten Rosemary, but she obviously had not forgotten me.

Becoming lost in the words in the letter, I failed to see my buddy Clarence who had come up behind me. Glancing over my shoulder with a cigarette hanging from his lips, he noticed that the return address on Rosemary's letter included the words, 'Reading, Pennsylvania.' "Who the hell do you know in Reading?" he blurted into my right ear, startling me back to the present. "An old girlfriend," I told him, "from my hometown." It was then that we found out for the first time that he and I lived in the same hometown. Clarence and I were going home together, and we were overjoyed.

When the Bienville arrived just outside Boston Harbor on the first of November, a large tugboat came out to greet us. It was filled from front to back with WACs and they sang to us. I don't remember if they sang well or not, but we thought they sounded wonderful. After all, anything sounded better than bullets.

After we docked and unloaded, we were taken to Camp Miles Standish near Boston to be processed. Within a couple of days we were split up and shipped out to different forts and camps. From Boston, I was sent to Fort Indiantown Gap for a couple of days, mostly filling out paperwork, and from there I was discharged on November 6, 1945, and sent home.

41
I Re-Enlist

The war was over, and I was free to go home. Left behind were the best friends I ever had: Ted and Joe in Trinidad, George from Mississippi, Alf, Olaf, Arne, Clarence, and a few hundred others from the 99th in Europe, and Yeanni and Bjorg in Norway. There were others as well, men who made the ultimate sacrifice for their country and were left behind on the battlefields of Europe. Suddenly I felt very much alone. I had had no contact with my father for the last four years, and my mother was gone. The Army was the only home I had really ever known, and now that was behind me as well.

After making the decision to return to Reading, I hitchhiked all the way to my sister's home. Catching a ride was easy since I was in uniform and many people felt privileged to help out a soldier. On the way to Reading, I visited every VFW post I could find, getting drunk and sleeping on pool tables. I was irritable, cantankerous, and intimidating. No one said a word to me, they just let me be. I was confused and felt abandoned. After three days of binging, I caught my last ride home. I was a civilian now and it would prove to be a difficult transition for me.

Betty and Jack invited me to move into their small apartment with them, and I was grateful for a place to stay. I loved my sister and was happy to see her again. Jack had had a few close calls (landing on Omaha Beach on D-Day and barely escaping capture at the Bulge), but survived the war, arriving home shortly before I did. Our reunion was a joyous one; we had not seen each other since our chance encounter on a snowy hillside in Malmady.

Jack was an engineer for the Reading Railroad and was able to secure a job for me as a puddler. I know just what you're thinking; I had no idea what a puddler was either, until I reported for my first day on the job. Steam locomotives required a fire to heat the water and produce steam. As a puddler, I was responsible for breaking down and cleaning out the firebox when the engines came into the yard. Once the box was cleaned out, I had to shoot fresh coal in the box and get the fire started again. It was hot as hell in there, but it was a job, and I was lucky to have one.

Not long after I started my job as puddler, I was promoted to brakeman, front end to be specific. There was also a rear brakeman who rode in the caboose. Because I was the young, inexperienced guy, I rode up front in the engine. Sounds like they had things a little mixed up to me, but I wasn't about to complain. Riding up front in the engine was a treat. Seeing where I was headed was much more interesting that seeing where I'd been. The train traveled from Reading, Pennsylvania, to Wilmington, Delaware, stopping midway to remove some cars. As brakeman, it was my job to back those cars off. Brakeman was kind of a neat job, and I liked it, but it wasn't going to last.

Adjusting to civilian life was very difficult for me. I instinctively watched my back, and any loud noise, like the sound of a vehicle backfiring, sent me running for cover. I had nightmares and migraine headaches, and felt unsettled and edgy most of the time. I was getting progressively worse by the day, and I knew there was just one thing for me to do. I gave my notice to the railroad and re-enlisted in the Army. I was starting to feel a whole lot better already.

42
Learning to Fly!

Riding on the train, not as a brakeman this time, but as a paying passenger, I was headed to Philadelphia to be sworn into the U. S. Army for the second time. Having no clue what was in store for me in the near future, I knew one thing for certain; no one would be shooting at me. In Philadelphia I was processed quickly and assigned to Camp Campbell, Kentucky. After saying good bye to Betty and Jack, I boarded a passenger train for my leisurely trip to Kentucky. Though Betty and Jack were sorry to see me go, they understood completely.

Two days on a train was nearly enough to settle me down, and I arrived at Camp Campbell, Kentucky rearing to go. The Army was darned pleased to have me; not too many combat infantry veterans re-upped after the war. To my great disappointment, however, I was immediately put into a detachment of military police. I did not want to be an MP, but had no immediate choice in the matter. The Army thought they were doing me a favor, but there was absolutely no challenge patrolling the warehouses in Camp, or keeping hundreds of new recruits in control and out of trouble. Accustomed to patrolling for Nazis, I was afraid I might shoot somebody. I became bored and discouraged very quickly.

I had only one experience worth mentioning while I was an MP. I was called to the NCO club (non-commissioned officers) to break up a brawl. Some reserves, here for summer training, got into a fight with the regular army guys. They were drunk and unruly and gave me a hard time, cursing and threatening me. Well outnumbered, I pulled out my .45 and called for backup. Fortunately, no one was drunk enough to get himself shot.

About the time I was beginning to doubt the sanity of my decision to re-enlist, an interesting opportunity presented itself. A notice was posted in camp announcing opportunities that were available to veterans under the G.I. bill. A variety of educational choices was being offered to the men, including flight lessons. Learning to fly was exactly the challenge I was looking for.

After filling out the paperwork, I hopped in a Jeep and drove to Outlaw Field in Tennessee. Now, keep in mind the Kentucky/Tennessee border ran right through Camp Campbell, so in reality Outlaw Field was just on the other side of camp, a couple of miles, to be exact.

Outlaw Field was a small airport with grass field runways and a flight school for private instruction. I attended classes two to three times a week for training, depending on my schedule with the Military Police. There were six of us attending flight school, and our first few sessions were held in a classroom at the airport. Here we were taught the basics of flight.

After completing the initial training in the classroom, we spent several hours out in the field becoming familiar with the planes and the general surroundings. The planes were Aeronca Champions, a popular light aircraft with a single 65 horsepower engine. They had tandem seating instead of side-by-side seating and were painted bright yellow.

Upon completing our classroom and field sessions, we were assigned instructors. My instructor, Mr. Drawn, was a former fighter pilot who flew Corsairs off the deck of an aircraft carrier during WWII. The day I met him, he took me up in the air to familiarize me with the airplane and the surrounding countryside in reference to the airport. Although the plane could be flown from either seat, he piloted the plane from the rear seat. I sat in front. Steering the plane was done with a stick and was not as easy as it sounds.

My flying lessons started the next day. He flew the plane on take-off and up into the training area which was a triangular shaped area in the sky. We trained only in this area for obvious safety reasons. All our exercises, stunts, and maneuvers were always performed in this triangle.

My first flight lesson consisted of an overview of all the exercises that we would be learning, such as power stalls, power off stalls, figure 8's, and 720's (laying the plane on its side and making a complete circle). We also discussed how to make an emergency landing if we lost power, and how to safely take off and land the plane. My instructor performed each of these maneuvers to demonstrate them to me. Things were really looking up!

During my second lesson, I was instructed to hold the stick while my instructor flew the plane from the rear seat.

Although he had complete control of the aircraft, I was getting the feel of flying the plane by holding onto the stick. Each time we flew, he let me have more control and I soon mastered the stick. Talking me through each and every step of the way, I began to learn maneuvers.

Landings proved to be my downfall, though not literally, as long as Mr. Drawn was in the plane, but to say they were difficult for me was an understatement. On landing, I would bounce the plane, and he would have to recover for me. More than once he said to me, "Red, if you want to die, don't take me with you!" He often scolded me for my antics, but we would usually just laugh about it.

For reasons unknown to me, I never really thought I'd crash the plane. I felt certain that I could land anywhere, anytime, in s pite of the fact that I hadn't done a successful landing even once. On a whim I once attempted to land in a potato field, scaring the hell out of my instructor. "No!" he screamed, pulling hard on the stick in an attempt to recover, "You can't land in a potato field, you'll kill us both!" Fortunately, he quickly recovered the plane, and just in the nick of time because I had completely lost control from laughing so hard.

Every lesson was a new adventure. One day my landing approach was too fast and too high and I was headed for a landing in the trees. After a quick recovery, he said, "Red, you are as nervous as a pregnant nun!" I laughed all the way through my next approach which, by the way, was bumpy, but landed us safely.

One day, however, I nearly tore the wings off the plane while doing a power stall. Flying full power, I brought the nose of the plane up into a gradual climb until the plane was almost vertical. The climb caused the motor to stall, and then I allowed the plane to roll over into a spin, heading straight down. I continued my dive until the propeller started, restoring power to the engine. Then I pulled back on the stick to bring us out of the dive. So far, so good. We were still alive. However, when pulling out of my dive, I gave the plane full throttle, a dangerous and often fatal mistake. Once again my instructor recovered for me, but I wasn't laughing this time because he was really mad. "Goddamn it, Red," he said, "You almost tore the wings off my goddamned airplane!"

By now, the other guys had done their solos, and I was feeling ready. Today, after completing my eleventh hour in the cockpit, I landed the plane and pulled over to the gas tanks to refuel. My instructor said, "Red, give me your license, you are on your own!" He instructed me "to take off, circle the airport twice, and land." Then he promptly got out of the plane, and I taxied to the runway and took off.

I could see Mr. Drawn and the men who had already done their solos standing on the grass field watching patiently. My instructor was confident that I would pull this off; the others were waiting for me to make a landing in the trees. Watching also was a Master Sergeant who had soloed before any of us. He was a brazen fellow, not well liked, and let me know that he did not like me.

With my hand on the stick, and just enough throttle, I took off by the seat of my pants, reveling in the sheer joy of flight. Once airborne, however, the realization kicked in that I was alone. My instructor wasn't going to save my ass this time. Following orders, I circled the airport twice, and then made a perfect landing, barely feeling the touchdown. I was damned proud of myself as I taxied over to the gas tanks and got out of the plane.

My audience was clapping and cheering, all except the Master Sergeant who was complaining to the instructor that my landing was one of the worst landings he had ever seen. Mr. Drawn looked at him and said, "You'll never live long enough to land a plane like he just did." I had actually learned to feel my landings, bringing down my tail wheel first, the way planes landed on aircraft carriers, tail first, catching the hook which stops them. Now I was hooked, and I could fly!

43
Fort Ord, California

Shortly after my solo at Outlaw Field, another opportunity presented itself. Men with combat infantry experience were being given the opportunity to transfer to any infantry unit they chose. I saw in this an opportunity to put my MP days behind me, and seek out a better climate. I had always wanted to go to California, and this was my chance. So I immediately put in for a transfer and was sent to Fort Ord near Monterey, as part of the Third Infantry Division, M Company.

My flight training continued here at Presidio Airfield, near Monterey, doing cross-country flights. Presidio was primarily a commercial airport, but was used by the military as well. My cross-country training involved hours-long flights without the use of a radio. I used an altimeter and compass and flew by visuals only. Even though the planes I flew were equipped with radios, I was not yet licensed to use one.

I flew 'by the tower,' which meant when approaching the airport I would look down at the tower, and they would give me a light. If they gave me a red light, I knew I had to circle the airport again. A green light meant bring the plane in for a landing. Once I was given a signal, I was expected to gently wave the wings of my aircraft to acknowledge that I had gotten the signal.

Returning one day from a flight, I approached the tower for a signal and was given a flashing green light. Even though I was not familiar with that signal, I surmised that I should proceed to land, but do so quickly. As it turned out, my intuition was right. I gave the plane a little extra power and landed it quickly. As I taxied off the runway, I saw that a commercial liner had come in for a landing just behind me and right on my tail!

Flying brought me many joys and even more adventures. I remember being lost once in fog. The fog was so thick on one return trip from a cross country flight that I couldn't see the airport. The front had moved in suddenly from the ocean. There was just one main runway, going east-west, and I couldn't find it, so I flew up the coast a short distance and found an opening in the clouds. Realizing that I was at Salinas Airport, I made a landing, called Presidio, and asked to speak to my instructor. When he picked up the phone, I heard an angry voice ask, "Where the hell are you?" I gave him my location and explained why I'd landed the plane. He was really angry and told me, "Get the hell back here now; fly that plane below the ceiling." Accustomed to following orders, I immediately took off and headed south in fog as thick as clam chowder. This is not the first time I'd been ordered to perform a dangerous task; I had done so many times in the past.

Flying by the seat of my pants, I guessed when I was close to the airport, then slowly made my descent through the thick mist, flying blindly for a few tense minutes until I suddenly broke through the cover and all was clear again. My altimeter indicated that I was a precarious five hundred feet off the ground, and located dead center between two mountains that lined each side of the runway. The minimum altitude for landing here was a thousand feet, but fortunately, my intuition saved the day.

I was quite notorious for entertaining the men by performing stunts over the runway, diving and stalling, catching hell from my instructor more than once. Flying was a wonderful release for me, and I eventually earned my Private Pilot's License.

When I first arrived at Fort Ord, I reported to Company Headquarters and was asked by the Company Commander what I knew about machine guns. I explained that I was quite knowledgeable with these weapons and many others as well and had used them frequently in combat. I was told to report to one of the supply areas to have a look at a 50-caliber machine gun. The weapon was sticking and could not be taken apart. I quickly identified the problem, easily disassembled the weapon, and carefully placed each part on the floor, explaining each step of the process. I was promoted from Pfc. to Buck Sergeant right on the spot, skipping Corporal completely. Things were looking up.

Not too long after the Sergeant stripes were added to my uniform, I was asked what I knew about close order drills, manual of arms, bayonet drills, and all the rest. My brief reply in the affirmative was exactly what they wanted to hear. I immediately became a drill instructor, and I was good at it.

I taught the new recruits all the drills and worked them hard. They learned close order drills which covered marching, manual of arms, and bayonet drills. Straw stuffed dummies served as targets for the recruits as they learned how to handle a bayonet as a combat weapon. We covered camouflage techniques and ran obstacle courses. I taught the men map and compass reading in a classroom setting, and they quickly became proficient, learning to orient themselves when practicing in the field. I was very experienced in the subjects I taught and soon became very proficient at teaching as well.

The Army was happy to have me, and they let me know it. Because most of the soldiers went home when the war ended, the Army lacked experienced men, and I was combat veteran. I could teach these young men things that could someday save their lives. I was one of the few instructors at Fort Ord with actual combat experience. The men respected me because of it, and I treated my recruits with a great deal of respect as well.

Every thirteen weeks I was given a new group to instruct, usually one Company, a few hundred men plus officers. I worked them hard but treated them fairly. I never screamed at them, attempting to set a good example. I was proud of them all. They looked up to me greatly because I had combat experience, and not one of the men ever gave me any trouble, except for minor infractions, which I'll describe. Drill instructor was a tough job, but I loved it.

One new recruit made the mistake of requesting an additional fifteen minutes of sleep when I walked into the barracks for the usual 4:00 AM wake up call. I flipped on the lights and shouted, "Everybody up, you got five minutes to get yourselves dressed." Blankets went flying into the air as men scrambled for their clothing and boots. Only occasionally (at least one man in each new group of recruits) did one of these young men dawdle, like the lad who asked for fifteen more minutes of sleep. "Sorry that I disturbed you, son, go right ahead," I said as I grabbed the frame of his bunk with two hands, lifted it off the ground, and tossed it completely over, its occupant landing hard on the floor with a thump. This violation never occurred twice in the same Company.

Talking among themselves while I was instructing earned the offenders a weekend on KP duty. Scrubbing pots and pans, and peeling potatoes and onions by the hundreds was good therapy and the men rarely needed a second treatment.

Before long, I was giving advice to the lovelorn, first one man, and then another. The recruits found in me a 'father figure' I suppose, and came to me with all kinds of problems, often involving women. "Hey Sarge," one young soldier said, "Since I joined the Army my girl wants to break up with me. What should I say to her?" "If she loves you, she'll wait," I remember saying to him and to dozens of other recruits over the next year. Some of the guys brought their "Dear John" letters for me to read; I felt bad for them, really bad. I advised them to keep their minds on their training because someday they might be involved in a conflict and need every bit of training in order to survive. As it turned out, many of the young men I trained eventually went off to fight in Korea.

"How would you like a week off, Sergeant?" my company commander asked me early one morning. "Sure," I replied, "what's up?" "Fort Leavenworth is holding one of our AWOLs from A Company; do you want to make the pickup?" Eager for a break to get the hell away from the exhausting routine of drilling newcomers, I agreed immediately. "I'll assign a Corporal to go with you," he informed me.

In just a few days my travel arrangements were made and Fort Leavenworth was informed of my exact arrival. Armed with .45 caliber pistols and paperwork for the release of the prisoner, Corporal Jim Peterson and I left Salinas, California for San Francisco, then on to Fort Leavenworth, Kansas, by train.

Two days later we were picked up at the railroad station by military police and taken to the fort, where we settled in for the night. After breakfast the next morning Peterson and I reported to the prison, the largest military prison in the country. The prisoner, a young man about nineteen years old with a bad attitude, was brought to me in handcuffs. Upon signing my name to documents placed before me, the Private became my responsibility. I informed him that he was now under my supervision and that he was, whether he liked it or not, going back with me to Fort Ord to face a military court martial. I told him, "Do not talk to me or the Corporal at any time during the trip, no smoking, no talking to other civilian or military personnel, and I will choose your meals." "Do you have any questions," I asked looking him directly in the eyes. His reply to me was a flat, "no."

En route to the train station the prisoner spoke to me. "Sergeant, I have something to say," he said, "don't think you are taking me back to Fort Ord; you will never get me back there." Looking directly at him I said, "You will either walk into Fort Ord, or you'll be carried in, it's you choice."

On our return trip to Fort Ord, shortly after taking our seats, the conductor approached me and said, "You may not handcuff this man to any part of this train. It's against regulations. Either uncuff him from the train or I will have you removed at the next stop." I replied, "If you attempt to remove us from this train, you will be reported to the United States Army and will have to answer to them." Before he could respond, a well dressed man approached us from the rear of the car, removed a wallet from his breast pocket, and identified himself as an F.B.I. agent. Slowly refolding his billfold, he looked directly at the conductor and said, "You will not put the Sergeant and his prisoner off this train. He may handcuff the prisoner anyway he chooses." Before I could open my mouth to thank the agent, he shook my hand and took his seat.

I kept the prisoner handcuffed at all times. By day he was handcuffed to the Corporal; by night he was handcuffed to the armrest of his seat. In a precautionary measure, I took the Corporal's .45 and kept it in my satchel. The prisoner gave me no trouble; and in return I gave him a few cigarettes. He was a pathetic kid and I felt sorry for him.

Around the time I returned from Kansas with the AWOL, I learned that wild fires were burning out of control north of San Francisco. Our commanding officer informed us that we were needed to help get the fires under control. The military was asked for the loan of four companies of men, who were transported by truck to within a few hundred yards of the fire.

Given chain saws, shovels and rakes, we were instructed to build a 'fire break,' a clear path wide enough to prevent the fire from spreading, by removing trees, brush and other vegetation that might burn. The forestry department supervised our work, 800 men approximately. We slept on the ground and kitchen trucks supplied us with meals. The work was hard, and the heat from the fire at times was intense. The fire illuminated the night sky stretching for miles across the horizon. Because we worked long hours, every opportunity we had to rest was spent in a prone position. Though the work was exhausting, I found this to be an interesting, though difficult, experience.

44

Task Force Williwaw
Adak, Aleutian Islands

World War II taught us many lessons; one of which was that the American soldier was ill-equipped to fight in bitter cold temperatures. The Soviets were very experienced arctic fighters, whereas the Americans were not, and deteriorating relations between the two nations brought to light the possibility of a future conflict. With war so fresh in their minds, the Army sought to ready its forces for winter operations in the arctic. In order to achieve this goal, a decision was made to establish a task force exclusively for the testing of military equipment, weapons, vehicles, and clothing. Human endurance in a sub-zero environment would be tested as well.

Three Task Forces soon became a reality, and I volunteered for the worst one of all. Task Force Frost was destined for Camp McCoy, Wisconsin; Task Force Frigid went to Alaska; and Task Force Williwaw was sent to Adak, Aleutian Islands, in the Bering Sea. I went to Williwaw. I volunteered to expose myself to harsh winter conditions, to test weapons, clothing and vehicles, and freeze my ass in sub-zero weather. What the hell was I thinking! Perhaps had I known the meaning of williwaw (a violent squall), I'd have stuck with training recruits on the balmy coast of California.

One Company of volunteers assembled at Fort Ord, California, sometime in September of 1946. I remember we were each given a Zippo lighter by the manufacturer who told us, "You'll never light a match in those winds." He was right about the matches, but the lighters were ineffective as well. We shipped out to Adak on an old freighter that had been refitted to carry troops, taking with us tanks, weasels, and an assortment of weapons and gear, including some interesting prototypes.

We arrived in Adak at the onset of its winter season, and the weather was already very cold and windy; thirty mile per hour winds on a good day, 150 mile per hour winds on a bad day. And we only had six months to go! Reminding myself that I had volunteered for this task force, I was already cold, but the vast stretch of tundra visible from the bow of our ship held opportunities for me. Ready for whatever lay ahead, I felt excitement welling up inside me.

We fell quickly into a routine, spending twenty days a month out in the field testing, and the remaining ten days recovering in camp. In the field we slept in sleeping bags, removing only our boots at night. However, we pulled our boots and weapons into our sleeping bags at night to prevent them from freezing. The weather was frequently stormy with rain, sleet, and snow, and more often than not precipitation fell horizontally due to high winds, hitting us directly in the face.

We had toboggans and sleds to carry our weapons and ammunition. These vehicles were equipped with harnesses that we draped over ourselves to transport our machine guns and equipment over the tundra. Vehicles carried some supplies, but most of the burden was borne by the men. We had no sled dogs to help us, only 'dog faces.'

A big part of our job was testing prototypes. I was involved in testing a carbine rifle equipped with a night scope that gave us the ability to see in pitch darkness. This was a new concept, and not without a few drawbacks. In order to operate the scope, a battery pack had to be carried along like a backpack. Heavy as hell, we were only allowed to carry the battery for a few days, and then hand it over to someone else. Prolonged exposure to the pack was thought to make men sterile. The scopes soon proved to be fairly useless because we could only see objects that were about 15 yards away.

The biggest problem we encountered with weapons was accuracy in firing them any distance due to the winds. I remember test firing a rifle, a sniper-type weapon, which was equipped with a vertical and horizontal floating sight. The device was designed to compensate for wind, but it also proved worthless. We tested many of the more basic types of infantry weapons such as rifles and machine guns, as well as lubricants, and gun barrels composed of various types of steel.

We took with us a couple of tanks and some T-15 Weasels. The weasels were originally developed for use by the First Special Service Force to support their winter operations. Weasels were all terrain vehicles, highly versatile under less harsh conditions. They were considerably more practical than tanks, maneuvering through water as well as traveling on land. In fact, they floated! I remember observing a weasel as it crossed over a little area of backwater. Someone apparently had not plugged it up properly, and the vehicle began taking on water, sinking before reaching the other side. All that remained of the weasel was a slender antenna sticking up out of the water. I'm certain someone caught hell for that!

We brought along a couple of tanks for testing but they proved to be completely useless, repeatedly getting stuck in mud and crevices. Corporal Willy Thompson was one of the tank drivers. He'd pop his head out the hatch and scream and curse every time he got stuck. "Goddamn bucket of bolts," he'd shout. We found his frustration and antics humorous, and laughed at him which did little to improve his mood.

Willy had always wanted to be a soldier, and to his great disappointment didn't turn eighteen until just about the time the war ended. But he enlisted in the Army anyway and was sent to Fort Ord for basic training, then learned to drive a tank. Our paths didn't cross until we shipped out for Adak and were out in the field one day testing the tanks.

Because Willy and I had a lot in common, we became fast friends. We both had a zest for life (that's what got us here), and there wasn't much we wouldn't attempt. We were also prone to monkey business in our free time, but Willy proved to be the master of mischief, especially when he'd had too many beers. The Army issued each man in the Task Force a monthly ration of one case of beer or one case of Coca Cola, but I don't remember ever seeing Coca Cola the entire time we were on the island. One case of beer may not seem like a lot, but we were only in camp 10 days a month, and Willy finished his off well before the ten days expired.

Willy got really drunk one evening, climbed into his tank, and began playing war. None of the guys in our hut noticed he had slipped away briefly until we heard the roar of a tank in the distance. We'd had a few beers that evening and had begun to settle into our bunks for the night when Willy stepped out. The thought never occurred to me that he might have gone for a joyride until the gun on his tank burst clear through our Quonset hut door, dead center making a big hole and just barely missing our little oil-fired stove. Another few inches and Willy would have blown us up; another few feet and he'd have taken down the hut burying us all in debris.

In spite of the fact that he could easily have killed us, we heard him laughing as he lifted the hatch and shouted at us. "Put your hands up and surrender right now or I'll blow you all to hell," he stuttered, laughing deliriously by now. "Okay," I replied, "We give up, don't shoot." Fairly certain that Willy wouldn't fire the gun we played along with him anyway and thrust our arms high into the air. Then a few of the men and I quickly jumped up on the turret, subdued Willy, and helped him get the tank back where it belonged. When the tank was safely returned, we brought Willy back to the hut, tossed him in his bunk, and let him sleep it off.

The next morning, Willy's full bladder woke him early. Mumbling, he pulled himself up and sat on the edge of his bunk trying to get his bearings. "It's cold as hell in here," he grumbled through his hangover, rubbing the sleep from his eyes. Rising slowly, he shuffled towards the exit, stopping dead in his tracks in front of a gaping hole in the door and asked, "What the hell happened here?" "Tell you about it later, buddy," I replied chuckling to myself over the events of last evening, then pulled the blanket up around my ears and went back to sleep.

Testing human endurance and tolerance was the most difficult challenge we would have to endure in Adak. However, after living in foxholes, hungry and cold during one of the worst winters Belgium had experienced in many years, I felt that no challenge in Adak could even come close to that. And I was right. Our endurance would be tested, but it would just be one big adventure for me.

One test involved digging a vertical fox hole, about three feet square and five feet deep, with picks and shovels, a challenge in itself for some men. About twenty holes were dug, two men assigned to a hole. Each hole was just large enough for two men, one man standing with his head above the top on constant lookout, and the other man sitting on an earthen seat with his feet squarely in front of his body and butted up against the man who was standing. To say that quarters were 'close' is a gross understatement and the test required the men to stay in the hole for 48 hours. To make matters worse, proximity wise, we had our rifles with us and our packs containing K-rations, toilet paper and bags for catching body waste, and a canteen of water. We had cigarettes and our Zippo as well. Keep in mind that I volunteered for this!

My companion, Corporal Harry Bergman, and I alternated resting and standing every one to two hours. Resting was relatively easy when compared to standing, as we became exhausted from being wedged in one spot, unable to move, and dropped off to sleep easily. I struggled to 'jog in place,' trying to keep my circulation going, but found myself repeatedly stepping on Harry's boots. "Hey, buddy, I need a little rest," we'd tell each other. We always switched when one of us was exhausted.

Keep in mind, the days were bitterly cold, but the nights were worse. Snow and sleet fell the whole 48 hours, precipitating horizontally, of course, hitting at least one of us in the face. Our clothes were 'prototypes,' state-of-the-art you might say, designed to keep us warm. Those 48 hours in the hole taught us that technology had a hell of a long way to go before military personnel would have proper clothing to survive in sub-zero weather.

We ate K-rations and drank coffee which we heated very carefully over Canned Heat. The Canned Heat warmed us just slightly but we discontinued using it when the gas pains kicked in. "Hey Serge," Harry inquired, "Did you just fart?" "Sorry, buddy," I replied, "just couldn't hold it." It wasn't too long before Harry's flatulence kicked in as well, the stench overwhelming us. We were cold that first night but neither one of us wanted to take a chance lighting our Canned Heat. We were certain we'd have blown ourselves up!

I was accustomed to relieving myself in foxholes, forests, and the battlefields of Europe, but performing bodily functions in a bag in such close proximity was awkward. Not just from a privacy standpoint, but physically awkward as well. So Harry and I somehow managed to 'hold it' until we were taken from the hole. We did, however, urinate in bags which we promptly placed outside the hole. Familiarity does, perhaps, breed contempt, because Harry and I got along just fine in the hole, but we socialized very little afterwards.

The whole time the men were 'dug in,' we were closely monitored, occasionally having our pulse and blood pressure taken. Men, posted to watch us, questioned us often, asking, "Hey, Sergeant, you OK? What about you, Corporal?" Our response was always the same, "It's damn cold in here," we'd inform him, and he'd go to the next hole and ask the same question. I guess he figured that a man who complains is still breathing, and a man who is breathing must still be alive.

When our 48-hour shift finally ended, we were so stiff that we had to be lifted out of the hole. Physically unable to climb out by ourselves, two men lifted each of us out of the hole and laid us on the ground. We were checked over again to be certain we were okay, and then permitted to crawl into a sleeping bag and pass out. I am not certain what the test results taught the Army, but it taught me to be a little more careful the next time I volunteered!

Camping out in the tundra was uncomfortable all of the time, but we were given some perks; for example, we were given a boost in rank. I went from Buck Sergeant to Staff Sergeant. Also, our ten days per month in base camp, resting and recuperating, were not completely devoid of entertainment; I have some interesting memories.

My bunkmates and I took into our Quonset hut a stray dog that had been wandering around the base alone. We began by tossing him meat, and before long he became our pet. He was a scrubby looking mixed breed about eighteen inches tall, with a long black and white coat. Quite often he'd go off and not come back for a few days. After running off several times, we decided to name him AWOL.

Quite comfortable in his new home, AWOL squatted one morning and left a nasty little pile on the floor of our hut. Annoyed with him, one of the guys picked him up and tossed him out the window into the snow. AWOL seemed to have a difficult time with the concept of "no crapping on the hut floor," and kept repeating his ill-mannered behavior, getting tossed out the window each time.

One day he came into the hut, looked cautiously at us, squatted, crapped, and leapt hastily out the window. He stood outside in the snow peering in at us, as though seeking our approval, quite proud of himself actually. He had finally mastered the program by doing exactly what we had taught him. Realizing that he was quite an intelligent dog after all, it was we who had a lot to learn about housebreaking a dog.

Months later, AWOL went missing and never returned to the hut. We all missed him, but not his antics. He was a fine pet, the only dog I ever saw in Adak, and sadly, we never saw him again.

Shivering from the cold provided all the physical exercise I needed, so I rarely visited the small gym in camp. Some of the guys played ball and I joined in occasionally, tossing a basketball into a hoop, or playing ping pong, but generally I wasn't interested; I preferred to be outdoors. We also had a small movie house called the Husky Theatre that seated about fifty men. I went there occasionally and saw some old movies, but wasn't too interested in movies either. Watching a movie involved too much sitting, and that was not something I did very well.

We had access to a few Canadian bobsleds which we used primarily to haul our equipment to and from the field. Each sled held about half a dozen men and sledding was a great way for us to let off steam. We controlled the sleds with our bodies, leaning left or right to turn, but stopping them was an entirely different matter. Freely lending its hills, the island was a wonderful playground, and we took full advantage of every opportunity to enjoy it. Although we suffered a few mishaps, bobsledding in Adak was a lot of fun.

We had a small PX that sold watches, gifts to send home, and personal items. On impulse, I purchased a beautiful 18K gold watch for myself, a Tuxedo Bulova, the first time I ever treated myself to something extravagant, and a hand-carved ivory scrimshaw pin for my sister. The pin, depicting Huskies and a pure gold nugget in a sled, was hand carved in Alaska of walrus tusk. I also sent a toy tank to my sister's son, John, which was inscribed with the names 'Willy' and 'Red.' Sadly, I lost the watch in San Francisco when a buddy and I got drunk. We were 'rolled' and robbed by a couple of guys at the International Settlement; the only time in my life I ever lost a fight. My nephew, John, enjoys the tank to this day, and my daughter, Sharon, treasures the pin, passed down to my wife, Helen, then to my daughter.

Fishing was truly my favorite pastime, not just Adak, and I spent most of my free time in pursuit of salmon. Willy loved to fish, as well, and we fished most often with hand lines, using bits of meat from mussels that grew all over the rocks. My technique was successful, and I frequently supplied the mess kitchen with a variety of fresh fish.

Spear fishing for salmon provided Willy and me another source of entertainment by adding a greater degree of difficulty to the sport. Our spears were double pointed with a burr on each end, firmly holding our catch in place. Many small inlets lined the coast where hundreds of salmon gathered in pools, making them easy prey for the hunter that I had become. Exploring the magic that was Adak fostered my love of fishing. It all began here in this barren but peaceful wilderness.

We ate well here in Adak. In addition to many varieties of fresh fish, we ate a lot of King Crabs, which we called spider crabs. Mussels, another local treat, were readily gathered from the rocks along the coast, put into a pot with seaweed, and cooked over an open fire; a delicious treat, even though we did not have any butter!

Although I was not a 'loner,' I enjoyed having time to myself, probably more so than the average guy. Even though I occasionally set out alone to fish, I was never without a companion. A small head would inevitably pop out of the water curiously keeping an eye on me while I fished. I learned a lot about seals that winter, mostly that they are naturally curious, very intelligent, and amazingly patient creatures, qualities that we should all aspire to. There was an abundance of seals, many of whom found me a fascinating study. The only other wildlife I recall seeing in Adak was ravens.

Ravens are large-bodied birds, larger than a chicken, with a long tail, and are fascinating to watch, especially during take off. The birds run for a distance while flapping their wings in order to get airborne, a task that appeared quite difficult for them. Since little or nothing grew on the Adak tundra, I often wondered what they found to eat in such a barren wilderness. I learned later that ravens are omnivorous, possessing the ability to survive on almost anything, including insects, grains, reptiles and carrion. Ravens, though seemingly ordinary creatures, are really quite extraordinary, and observing their antics taught me to look at the world just a little more closely.

Active volcanoes lined the entire Aleutian chain, often rumbling beneath us as we lay in our sleeping bags, the rhythmic vibrations lulling us to sleep. On a few occasions, however, while lying deeply asleep in my cot at camp, I was abruptly awakened as a sudden eruption shook me firmly in my bunk. I soon became at ease with these natural occurrences, and eventually found the activity comforting. One of nature's melodies, I called it, just one more of natures many miracles.

After spending a long, cold winter in Adak, the Army abruptly cut short our stay when we became trapped in a ravine at the Bay of Islands. Trapped for a couple of days by a very severe storm, I now fully understood the meaning of the term williwaw. We were conducting tests on weapons in very high winds that day, when a storm moved in quickly, bringing with it 150 mile per hour winds. Our eighty pound packs and most of our equipment were swept away instantly. Even the weasels couldn't retrieve us.

Nearly freezing to death, we remained huddled closely together in the ravine until the storm blew over and the winds eventually subsided enough to permit us to walk out on our own and return to camp. Our walk back to camp after the storm warmed our frozen limbs only slightly; at least the exercise got our circulation going again. The weather was bitterly cold and the winds slowed us down, but the thought of bunking down by the little stove in our Quonset Huts kept us moving.

I felt like I was sleeping in a four-star hotel when I climbed into my bunk that evening. The oil-fired stove, built from a barrel, felt more like a roaring fire, and the chorus of guttural sounds coming from a score of sleeping men was a symphony compared to the roar of a williwaw. I was exhausted. Life in the Army was good to me; never a dull moment, I thought to myself, as I drifted off to sleep. I needed my rest, as daybreak would inevitably bring with it my next adventure.

After breakfast the next morning, we were told that Task Force Williwaw had fulfilled its mission, and that we would all be going back to the States. The Army concluded that if any enemy attempted to attack the west coast of the United States through the Aleutian Islands, they would never survive the climate. But before we went back to our huts to pack our things, we were asked if we would be willing to volunteer for a desert warfare task force.

Having had enough adventure for now, I had no difficulty stifling my impulse to volunteer. Six years in the Army had finally taught me to choose carefully, and this was only the second time that I did not volunteer. With my luck, I'd have ended up in Death Valley. To the great disappointment of the Army, no one volunteered for the desert task force. We all had had enough.

The trip back to Fort Ord was rough. Soon after leaving Adak, we sailed into a bad storm, and high rolling seas made a lot of the men sick. Everyone was relieved when we made a brief stop in the small town of Whittier, Alaska, in Prince William Sound. I believe we may have picked up men from Task Force Frigid there, but I am not certain. The scenery while sailing into Whittier was a breathtaking mix of passageways, rocky shores, and glaciers. Millions of years of glaciations had contributed to the many beautiful tributary fiords and islands. I was awed by its majesty.

The weather in the Sound was windy and bitterly cold that day, but with good visibility, a respite compared to the voyage from Adak. We did not disembark at Whittier but were free to relax on deck, fish or enjoy the scenery. A few of the guys rounded up some meat from the galley for bait and some heavy duty hand lines. I had a memorable and successful afternoon fishing in the pristine waters of Prince William Sound, dining on fresh Sole that we caught from the deck of our ship that beautiful day in Alaska.

45
Back to Fort Ord

When I returned from Task Force Williwaw in March of 1947, I immediately resumed my duties as drill instructor at Fort Ord, California. Although a new batch of recruits every thirteen weeks kept me busy, I had a lot of free time on my hands, so I purchased an outboard motor, a 5-1/2 HP Elgin, which I kept at a dock in Monterey. Almost every weekend I went down to the dock, often with Willy, and had a meal of seafood or abalone. Then I'd rent a boat and go out on the bay sightseeing and fishing. My little Elgin took me quite a distance as I followed the coastline, accompanied by a few curious sea lions. Those were pleasant times motoring and fishing along the beautiful Monterey coastline.

One day while motoring around on the water, I was astounded by the sight of a submarine that had just surfaced in the Bay. I hadn't realized that the water in Monterey was so deep until that day. Eventually I saw other submarines surface in the Bay during my stay in Monterey.

Eventually I bought a car, a Model A Ford that I had admired for some time. A buddy of mine who was being discharged from the Army sold me the car for $25.00. I used it mostly for taking in the scenery around Monterey and hauling my Elgin to and from the Bay, but the bugger left me sitting most of the time. The upside was that it provided me with a lot of exercise, because I had to push it almost as far as it took me.

We had a club here in Ford Ord that was built for military personnel, called the Million Dollar Service Club because it was financed by celebrities. The club sat on a hill overlooking Monterey Bay directly across the highway from Fort Ord. I frequently performed there, playing guitar and singing popular songs of the '30s and '40s. I must have been pretty descent because I always drew a crowd. Often when I went to the club just to have a drink, the guys persuaded me to get up and sing. "Hey Sarge," they'd shout, "Get up there and sing us a song." No one was happy unless I obliged. Because I enjoyed being up on stage singing my heart out, playing at the club was a treat for me. It was the beginning of a lifelong hobby, singing and playing guitar with my buddies, and later on with my wife, Helen, and daughter, Sharon, both of whom learned to play guitar.

In November that year, I was ordered to report to Regimental Headquarters to the commanding officer, a Colonel. When I arrived at his office, he informed me that I had been selected from thousands of men for a very special assignment, and the Army would be "very grateful" if I accepted. The army had given me many opportunities, and though this one would be difficult, it would prove to be one of the most memorable.

46
War Dead Escort

Because of shipping restrictions during the war, American military cemeteries overseas became a temporary burial place for Americans who died during the war. In May of 1946, Congress authorized the return of remains interred abroad for those families who wished to have their loved ones buried at home. After being shipped back to the States, the remains were loaded into railroad cars and taken home to the next of kin. Told that this was a highly important mission, an honor to be chosen, I proudly accepted the duty.

Before beginning escort duty, I was sent to class for two weeks. About to become a representative of the United States government, I was solely responsible for the dignified handling and safe delivery of the remains. I knew, too, that I would have to deal personally with bereaved families. I would have to be tactful and unaffected, conduct myself in an exemplary manner, and be impeccably groomed and dressed at all times. As a sign of deep respect, I had to wear a black brassard (armband) upon delivering the fallen soldier to his family.

I remember the first soldier I escorted home. His name was Sgt. John Bonvicino, and he had died in Toscana, Italy, on July 5, 1944. I attended his funeral service at the invitation of his family. We were gathered inside a large mausoleum. A single bugler stood outside the entrance of the mausoleum, and another bugler was stationed about half a block down the road. A firing squad stood in formation in front of the building.

At the end of the service, the funeral director and I folded the flag, and I handed it to a woman, the next of kin. I don't recall if she was a wife or mother of the deceased, but she was sitting on a marble bench inside the mausoleum. I got down on one knee and handed the flag to her and said, "I present you this flag as a token from a grateful nation." I was able to do this and retain my composure. Today I cannot even retell the story without getting emotional.

After handing over the flag, I stood up and saluted the coffin. The pallbearers picked up the coffin in a feet-first position and turned, facing the direction of interment. The firing squad fired three sets of volleys and the bugler at the entrance began to play taps, followed closely behind by the second bugler. I will never forget the sound of the bugles as the melody echoed off the marble walls of the mausoleum. Sgt. John Bonvicino was finally laid to rest on December 6, 1948, in his hometown in California.

There were others who I escorted to their final resting places. Those, too, involved attending funerals, and consoling grief stricken families. I remember one funeral where the deceased's mother would not speak to me, or even look at me. She was devastated to have lost her son, while I had the good fortune to survive. Having lost so much in my life, I completely understood her suffering. Ironically, even though I had survived the war, I had no mother to go home to.

My final duty as war dead escort was the most challenging and memorable one of all. I traveled by rail from San Francisco, California to Philadelphia, Pennsylvania with fifty-five war dead killed in the Pacific. The train made one stop in Chicago where the car was detached from the train and reattached to another train headed to Philadelphia. Because I was completely responsible for the safe delivery of the remains, I kept a very close eye on the men making the switch. The railroad required me to present a ticket for each of the deceased as well as one for me. As you can well imagine, I had pocket full of ticket stubs.

Always traveling in an adjoining car, I was able to make frequent inspections, checking to see that all was well. Every time the trained stopped, I'd make an inquiry as to the length of our stay, then inspect the boxes and make sure the shades in the car were still drawn. Sometimes the jostling motion of the train caused one or two of the boxes to shift or the shades to fly up. Drawn shades were the ultimate sign of respect.

After arriving in Philadelphia, I completed paperwork, handed the war dead over to the Army, and then boarded a train for my return trip to Fort Ord. This was my final mission for the United States Army, and I felt truly honored to bring these men home.

EPILOGUE

On February 11, 1949 I was honorably discharged from the United States Army for the second time, this time at Fort Ord, California, and returned home to Reading to begin a new life. I moved back in with my sister Betty and her husband Jack, and in August of the same year enlisted in the Army Reserves for three years.

Shortly after returning home, I received the sad news that my father had passed away. Even though we were together for only a short time, I suddenly missed him and couldn't help but wonder what our relationship might have been like.

Because of my logging experience while in the CCCs, I was hired to work for a construction company, cutting down timber and clearing brush to make way for heavy equipment. The equipment was removing coal waste from the Schuylkill River in Berks County, Pennsylvania. Coal mining operations in northern Pennsylvania were responsible for dumping water into the river that had been used to wash coal. The resulting runoff was loaded with culm, thus polluting the river and its tributaries.

As soon the river was cleaned up, I began an apprenticeship at Yocum Brother's Cigar Factory, eventually earning my journeyman's papers. Ultimately I became an Industrial

Mechanic, repairing large industrial machines for Firestone Tire and Rubber Company, a job I enjoyed for many years before retiring in 1984.

Four months after my discharge from the Army, on a warm May afternoon, I headed east in the 1100 block of Chestnut Street, in Reading to visit my good buddy, Willie Weller. Willie's sisters, Helen and Betty, were sitting on the steps of the front porch with their mother when I pulled up in my '36 Buick. I parked the car, got out and walked over to greet mom and the girls, one of whom was about to become my gal. Willie's little sister, Helen, had grown into a beautiful young woman with big blue-grey eyes and long thick curly brunette hair.

The girls were tickled pink to see me, but I only had eyes for Helen. I invited them both to go out for a coffee and they quickly agreed. Wasting no time, Helen headed directly for the front seat of the car and jumped in beside me, leaving Betty to sit in the back. We drove to the Sunset Diner in Exeter Township, drank coffee, and played the juke box. The girls were chatty, and we laughed a lot. Helen sat next to me in the booth, once again leaving Betty to sit by herself on the other side.

I found out that Helen's birthday was just a couple of days away, so I asked her to go out with me to celebrate her birthday. She happily accepted my invitation, and we went out on our official first date on May 8, 1949. She was 22 years old, and I was 25.

I bought her a bottle of perfume, a box of chocolates, and took her to the Boston Restaurant in downtown Reading. We had a wonderful time, and I soon introduced her to my sister, Betty. Betty and Jack became fond of Helen very quickly, but her brother, Willie, was not too happy with the arrangement. Even though Willie and I were good buddies, he didn't like the idea of me dating his sister. I was "too wild" he said, "too much drinking and fighting," not the kind of guy for his kid sister. I admit that I had earned quite a reputation for myself, but little did he know that love was just the cure-all I needed. When Helen walked into my life, I left the drinking and fighting behind forever.

Helen and I fell deeply in love, became engaged, and married on July 8, 1950, at First E. C. Church at 8th and Court Streets in Reading, Pennsylvania. During our 52 years of marriage, we had four daughters, five grandsons, five granddaughters, and great-grandchildren that are still arriving. Our family loved fishing, horseback riding, singing and playing guitar, and long rides in the country. We had many wonderful holiday dinners, lots of family get-togethers, and some really wonderful friends. Helen and I had a wonderful life together.

My beloved Helen, who had suffered from congestive heart failure for the last couple of years, passed away peacefully in her sleep on December 5, 2002, at the age of 75, after a very brief illness. My story is a written tribute to her—a selfless woman who brought joy and love to the lives of others.

The End

AFTERWORD

The reason for documenting my story is not entirely clear to me, except to say that I have felt the need for a very long time. I really wanted to forget, but the memories don't go away. Memories can be so distant, yet remain so vivid, especially those we try most to forget.

I had put pen to paper many times, at the encouragement of my wife, Helen, but could never truly find the right words, stopping and starting over many times. Finally, I put the notes in a drawer and let the idea rest for nearly sixty years, before discovering the medium to carry my most personal and profound experiences to written form was my daughter, Sharon. She inspired me to "let it go, send it out into the world," she said, in the belief that I could find peace, become free of remorse, and others might find peace in its message, as well.

The memories will remain with me always, but sharing my story with my daughter has lightened my burden, freeing me enough to allow a newly found sense of pride to emerge— the same pride I once felt as a young soldier serving with the 99th Infantry Battalion (Separate), a pride that summons fond memories of the men, whose names I can't recall, but whose faces and deeds, and acts of courage and comradery lift my spirit to this very day.

May your spirit be lifted as well.

Red Wells

CONTACT INFORMATION

If you would like to contact Red Wells, or the author, please feel free to do so by emailing us at the following address: SgtRedWells@gmail.com We hope to hear from you.

BIBLIOGRAPHY

Nyquist, Gerd. *99th Infantry Battalion (Separate).* H. Aschehoug
& Co. (W. Nygaard), Oslo, 1981.

Adleman, Robert H. and Walton, Colonel George. *The Devil's
Brigade.* Naval Institute Press, Annapolis, MD, 1966.

Kelly, Sgt. John. *Company D, United States Army.* Kirstes
Boktrykkeri, Oslo, 1945.

Department of the Army, *Escorting American War Dead.* August
1948.

National Archives. National Personnel Military Records.
Washington, D.C

Moody, Sidney C., Jr. and the Associated Press. *War In Europe.*
Presidio Press, 1993.

Reporting World War II, American Journalism 1938-1946. The
Library of America, 1995.

Keegan, John. *The Second World War.* Penguin Books, 2005.

Sledge, E. B. *With The Old Breed at Peleliu and Okinawa.* Oxford
University Press, New York and Oxford, 1990.

Illustrated Story of World War II. The Reader's Digest Association,
Inc. Pleasantville, New York, 1969.

99th Infantry Battalion (Separate). *Haakon VII Returns Home.*
Herald-Saga Newspaper, Vol. 1, No. 1. Norway, 1945.

Decade of Triumph The 40s. The Editors of Time-Life Books.
Alexandria, Virginia, 1999.

MAJ Doug Bekke, US Army retired. *Norwegian-Americans and*

the 99th *Infantry Battalion (Separate).* Curator, Minnesota Military Museum. The Military Historical Society of Minnesota.

Convoy Duty Top Secret for 25 Years, 99th Infantry Battalion Newsletter, Issue #4, March, 1997.

PHOTO CREDITS

Made in the USA